Information Users and Usability in the Digital Age

Information Users and Usability in the Digital Age

G. G. Chowdhury
and
Sudatta Chowdhury

Neal-Schuman Publishers, Inc.
New York

Published by Neal-Schuman Publishers, Inc.
100 William St., Suite 2004
New York, NY 10038

First published in the United Kingdom by Facet Publishing, 2011. This simultaneous U.S. edition published by Neal-Schuman Publishers, Inc., 2011.

Printed and made in the United Kingdom.

The paper used in this publication meets the minimum requirements of American National Standard for Information Sciences—Permanence of Paper for Printed Library Materials, ANSI Z39.48-1992.

ISBN 978-1-55570-807-8

Contents

Preface

It has become a common part of our everyday life to use a variety of online information products and services. These include e-mail and web services, search engines, mobile applications, library catalogues, scholarly databases and digital libraries. Online information services have existed for around 50 years. They appeared in the early 1960s providing facilities for remote access to online library catalogues and bibliographic databases of scholarly information comprising abstracts or full texts of journal and conference papers. Since then a significant amount of research and development activity has taken place to improve online information services. While some of these research activities focused on developing better information search and access mechanisms, others have focused on measuring the effectiveness and efficiency of online information databases and search services.

Early research on the evaluation of information retrieval systems focused on developing parameters for measuring the level of performance of various retrieval systems and techniques. Originally these evaluation experiments were based on small test collections, which were used to measure the performance of specific online databases or search systems. Subsequently the size of the test collections grew and the retrieval evaluation research became more robust, focusing on more complex retrieval algorithms and research problems. At the same time, research on human information behaviour focused on different research problems related to information needs and user behaviour, and the number of online information systems grew rapidly, giving rise to a large number of models on general human information behaviour, information seeking and retrieval. Thus progress in information systems and services has significantly benefited from systems- and user-centred evaluation research in information. Together this research aimed not only to assess the performance measures of various information retrieval systems based on certain specific retrieval measures, but also to understand information seeking and retrieval behaviour and patterns to address such questions as why certain systems perform better than the others, why users like or don't like certain system features, and so on.

The nature and characteristics of online information services have changed significantly over the past few decades and the pace of these changes has been extremely rapid and widespread as the internet has developed over the past two decades or so. Online information products and services were once designed for only a small subset of the population – academics, researchers and some policy-makers, who needed access to certain information in order to perform their tasks, make decisions, and acquire certain knowledge for enlightenment or pleasure. In today's world, online information products and services have become part of the everyday life of most of the population. Many people use online information to inform many activities in their daily lives. Information products and services range from conventional scholarly information accessible through library catalogues, electronic books, online databases, electronic journals and so on, to myriad websites and digital libraries providing access to information from millions of personal and institutional sources containing free and fee-based information. There are also a variety of mobile phone applications for performing specific tasks and activities, watching digital television, creating and sharing information on social networks and so on, each dealing with specific information products and services that are designed to meet specific user needs. The list of online information products and services appears to be endless, and while we purposely seek and use some of these information services – such as specific websites or databases – we use others indirectly, for example by accepting invitations from a Facebook friend, or through a specific mobile application.

Each of these online information products and services – be they in the form of websites, online databases, e-books or e-journals, social networking sites or mobile applications – is designed with specific business or other objectives and purposes to meet the specific needs of some users. These information products and services may be targeted at general or specialist users, for example academics, researchers or students, who need access to scholarly information; the general public, who need information about the government, health or politics; or specific mobile phone users or e-book readers.

Some online information products and services are designed and marketed purely for commercial purposes where the information product or service provider wants to make profits by charging customers directly through subscription or payment of fees for use, or indirectly where the cost of the service is recovered from the service provided, for example for online flight or holiday booking systems, or through advertisement revenues. Again, some online information products and services are designed by governments, institutions, international bodies or charities where the aim is to help people do their job more effectively and efficiently by using the online information service, or by learning more and thereby making informed decisions. Whatever may be the nature and objectives of an information product or service, and whoever may be the target audience or user, it is extremely important for designers and the product or service providers to know how the given product or service is meeting its stated objectives, how it compares with similar other products on the market, if any, what the target customers say and feel about the product, how to improve the product, and so on. This can be accomplished by conducting a usability study.

Although it has its root in early information retrieval system evaluation and user studies in general, usability as a field of study and research has been prevalent within the software engineering and human–computer interaction (HCI) community. Many new books on conducting usability studies in the context of software engineering and website design have appeared in the recent past, and some of them are cited in this book in one or more of the chapters. Like software engineers and software developers, every information professional in today's world – be they involved in the design of specific information products or services, engaged in providing information services, or involved in information research – needs to acquire the skills to conduct usability studies with a view to designing the product that suits changing and emerging user needs and meets the emerging standards of the evolving web and information and communication technology (ICT) marketplace. However, there are few books on usability written specifically for information professionals engaged in designing and/or providing online information services. This book aims to fill this gap. It is written primarily for information science researchers – practitioners and students – who want to get an overall idea of the field of usability study with special reference to conducting usability research on information products and services, digital libraries and so on. In addition to theoretical discussions on the concept of usability and user studies in the context of information science, the book discusses various tools, techniques and standards used for conducting these studies, supplemented by discussions on practical usability studies by the authors of this book and other researchers.

The book has ten chapters. A cover-to-cover reading will provide a comprehensive view of usability studies and it can be used as the starting point for conducting usability research in information studies. Some chapters may be read independently if knowledge on some specific aspects of usability studies is required. The first chapter presents some general information about usability and user needs studies, and by giving some examples of online information products and services, it builds a case for the need for a book on usability. Chapter 2 provides an introduction to some techniques and methods used to gather information about users, their information needs and information behaviour. It may be read alone, or perhaps better in conjunction with Chapter 3, which gives an overview of various information behaviour and information seeking and retrieval models. These two chapters present a general background and understanding of usability and user studies in information science.

Chapters 4, 5 and 6 may be read independently or together in order to acquire some basic skills for conducting usability research in information science. Although readers are expected to read the associated references in order to learn more about the specific tools, techniques and methods of usability studies, together these three chapters provide information and skills that are necessary to conduct research on the usability of any online information product or service. Chapter 4 discusses how to conduct a usability study at different stages of an information product lifecycle and provides various approaches, tools and techniques. Chapter 5 discusses how to select users when conducting a usability study and gives various sampling techniques and associated challenges. Thus Chapters 4 and 5 will teach readers about how to design a usability study, how to choose the study participants and how to collect data and so on. Chapter 6 discusses some basic quantitative and qualitative data analysis techniques necessary for statistical interpretation of usability research data.

Chapters 7 and 8 introduce readers to various web and digital library usability studies in order to provide an insight into different methods, techniques and tools that various information science researchers have used for conducting usability studies over the years within specific contexts. These two chapters can be read independently in order to get an overview of usability research in the information field with special reference to some specific tools, techniques and methods used for data collection within a specific research context, but when read in conjunction with chapters 4 to 6 they will offer skills and insights from practical research for conducting usability studies. They will guide an information science researcher in choosing the appropriate research technique relevant to the specific usability study context as discussed in these chapters.

Chapter 9 provides a broader context for usability research, giving a broad overview of some contemporary issues and challenges associated with the modern web and ICT environment and access and usage barriers. It discusses the concept and challenges of the digital divide, the divide created between different sections of our society from the inequality in the availability of, and/or access to, modern ICT and internet facilities. It also discusses the differences that exist among digital natives – those born since the 1990s who are ICT and internet savvy – and digital migrants – those born before the beginning of the ICT and internet revolution who have adapted themselves, to a greater or lesser extent, with everyday use of ICT and internet, in the context of today's information society. Thus Chapter 9 can be read alone to get an idea of the major challenges facing today's information world that have a bearing on the usability of information products or services. Reading this chapter in conjunction with reading the rest of the book will provide more insights for conducting usability research that would be appropriate for different sections of today's society.

Chapter 10 concludes the book with a brief discussion of the various issues and trends of usability research. It includes discussion of the major recent developments in the online information world brought by major players in today's digital information market ranging from Google and Amazon to Apple and Sony, each of which have been constantly developing new information products, services and applications, which have a significant impact on access to, and usability of, online information products and services. This chapter can be read independently in order to get an idea of the emerging issues and challenges in the information market in the context of usability of information products and services. However, reading it in conjunction with other chapters will give a usability researcher more understanding of the challenges and trends of research in usability and the emerging online information marketplace.

Acknowledgements

This book would not have been possible without constant help, support and encouragement from a number of people. We are thankful to Helen and her team at Facet Publishing, particularly Sarah Busby and Lin Franklin, for their constant support and help while we were writing this book. They have always been considerate of our personal circumstances, which brought inordinate delays in the publication process, and have provided support and encouragement. We are grateful to our two wonderful sons – Avirup and Anubhav – who have kept encouraging us while we were writing the book, despite at times not having as much attention as usual, when we were writing or discussing and debating several aspects of the book. We are grateful to various other members of our family – our parents, sisters and brothers – who have always given us encouragement and bestowed their good wishes.

Finally we would like to thank the following organizations whose websites we have used in the book in the form of screenshots to illustrate our discussions and justify our arguments:

- UK Parliament (www.parliament.uk/); Figure 1.1
- East Dunbartonshire Council (www.eastdunbarton.gov.uk/); Figure 1.2
- NHS UK (www.nhs.uk); Figure 1.3
- the BBC (www.bbc.co.uk); Figure 1.4
- BBC Children (www.bbc.co.uk/children); Figure 1.5
- the Library of Congress (www.loc.gov); Figure 1.6
- the British Library (www.bl.uk); Figure 1.7
- Europeana Digital Library (www.europeana.eu); Figure 1.8
- UTS Library (www.lib.uts.edu.au/); Figure 1.9
- University of Strathclyde Library (www.lib.strath.ac.uk/); Figure 1.10
- Oxford University Library (www.ox.ac.uk/); Figure 1.11
- MIT Libraries (http://libraries.mit.edu/); Figure 1.12.

We should also like to acknowledge with thanks the work of all other authors (all of whom are known to us personally), publishers and copyright holders of the figures and tables listed on the following pages. If there are any queries please contact Facet Publishing.

Figures and tables

Figures

Tables

1

Introduction

The main goal of an information service is to meet the user requirements for finding and accessing relevant information. In other words, users are, or at least should be, at the centre of any information service irrespective of whether it is free or fee-based, local or remote. Prompted by the introduction of computers in information processing in the late 1950s, a large variety of online databases and information search services began to be marketed in the 1960s. The rate of growth of local and remote online information services has increased significantly with the appearance and proliferation of the internet and the world wide web some two decades ago. Information services now play a major part in almost all our day-to-day activities in today's society.

However, information services existed long before the invention of computers. Traditionally, libraries provided information services, and libraries have existed for centuries. Users, and ease of use of information, were the two major driving forces behind these services. The importance of users in the context of library and information services was acknowledged by Ranganathan (1963) in his famous Five Laws of Librarianship in the 1930s:

- Books are for use.
- Every reader his book.
- Every book its reader.
- Save the time of the reader.
- A library is a growing organism.

It may be noted that although Ranganathan conceived these laws nearly a century ago in the context of libraries, they are very much applicable in today's electronic information world where one can easily reword these laws to state:

- Information is for use.
- Every user her [piece of] information.
- Every [piece of] information its user.
- Save the time of the user.
- Information is a growing organism.

In other words, while creating and/or managing an information service, we should always keep users in mind so that every bit of information stored within the system is accessible by its target users, and as a corollary users of the information system or service should find the information they require efficiently and effectively.

However, the importance of users and ease of use was recognized in the context of information services long before Ranganathan. For example, towards the end of the last century, Cutter explicitly mentioned that the objectives of a bibliographic system were (Cutter, 1904; Svenonius, 2001):

- to enable a person to find a book
- to show (a user) what the library has
- to assist (a user) in the choice of a book.

These three objectives of a bibliographic system proposed by Cutter – the finding objective, collocating objective and choice objective (Svenonius, 2001) – clearly put users and their needs at the forefront of an information system.

The notions of users, their information needs and ease of use of information have become more challenging, and therefore a central focus of research in the modern digital information age, mainly because we are often confronted with a variety of questions related to users and their needs, such as:

- Who are users of an existing or a proposed information service in the digital age, and how do we identify them, especially in the context of web information services where almost anyone anywhere in the world can be a potential user?
- How do we assess the needs of groups and those of individual users who may use an information system locally or remotely?
- How do we find out the characteristics of the information needs of users in a specific domain or environment, with a specific cultural and ethnic background?

- How do we assess whether or not an existing information system and its specific services meet users' requirements?
- How do we assess the information needs of users and how can we incorporate them in the design of a new information system so the resultant information services can meet the requirements of the target users?
- How should we keep track of the changing needs and behaviour of users in the rapidly changing world of information services, influenced by the rapid changes in information and communication technologies (ICTs) and the internet, so that we can adjust and improve the information services accordingly?
- How should we assess the needs of remote and future generation of users?
- Which factors influence users' information seeking and use behaviour and are they always the same or similar; if not, how do they change, temporally and spatially?
- What are the most appropriate methods and approaches to understand users and their requirements of information behaviour in the context of tasks and activities in their daily lives for which they may need information?
- What do we need to know to assess the impact of an information service on the life and activities of a user community?

These are complex questions, which are becoming more and more challenging because technology is changing very fast – and this has implications on user information behaviour and expectations – and virtually anyone anywhere in the world can be a potential user of an information service. Therefore information system designers and managers are facing an uphill task of meeting the needs of a user community a large number of whom may be unknown, unseen, and often have a different physical location, characteristics and nature of activities, language and culture, and so on.

The internet and the web have also changed the notion of information and its importance in our everyday life. Traditionally information access and use was primarily an activity that only a select few in our society participated in – those who were primarily engaged in academic and research activities, or in some specific professions like law or medicine. With the introduction and proliferation of the web, associated technologies such as mobile devices, social networking and so on, information has become a part of the daily life of almost everyone. In the course of our daily life and activities we access and use a variety of information systems and services ranging from communications, such as e-mail, to social networking, such as Facebook, to a myriad of web-based database systems and information services. Each of these information systems no matter how ubiquitous and unnoticeable – our washing machines, microwaves, cash tills – or how explicit – institutional web pages, library databases, airline and hotel booking systems, online shopping sites – has to meet the target users and their specific information needs, so the resulting information system can be easy to use and meet user requirements. Consequently users and usability of information systems have become a major area of study in different fields, from software systems and business management to different branches of engineering and system development, and all kinds of information services.

Information users

The Online Dictionary for Library and Information Science (ODLIS) (Reitz, 2007) defines the term 'user' as 'any person who uses the resources and services of a library, not necessarily a registered borrower'. Other terms often used synonymously with user include patron or client, but user is by far the most frequently used term.

Wilson (2008b, 457) commented that the concept of user 'has been of interest in librarianship and information science much longer than either has existed as a focus for research', and as an example he mentions the creation of the union catalogue of manuscripts in English monastery libraries in the late thirteenth century as a finding aid for scholar monks. Modern day examples of the importance of users in the context of library and information services may be found in the rules for dictionary catalogues proposed by Cutter (1904) over a century ago, and the central role of users in any library and information services was emphasized by Ranganathan in the famous Five Laws.

However, the first study of users in order to learn their information needs and behaviour was much later. Wilson (2008b, 457) notes that it took some time, 'before the "user" as a living, breathing person became the focus of attention in information research', and it began with the Royal Society Scientific Information Conference held in 1948, although the initial focus was on the system used.

Users in the web environment

Almost every information service – whether a digital library or scholarly information service, an online news service or a government information service – now uses the web for its information access and transaction services. Yet, information services are different in many respects, including their look and feel, design, interface and access features. A few examples of the websites of information services are shown here to highlight some significant differences between them and thus emphasize features relating to information users and the usability of online information services.

The UK Parliament website (Figure 1.1) is for the general public, primarily the British public, but anyone from anywhere can use it. Figure 1.2 overleaf shows the website of East Dunbartonshire Council, a typical local council in the UK; it specifically states that the page is primarily addressed to those

Figure 1.1   *UK Parliament website (www.parliament.uk/)*

Figure 1.2   *East Dunbartonshire Council website*
(www.eastdunbarton.gov.uk/)

living in East Dunbartonshire, but it may be of interest to other people as well. This website provides some interactive features that have a high level of security, for example those to make online payments of council tax and other services.

We can compare the content and presentation of the two websites shown in Figures 1.1 and 1.2 with that of another government website in the UK – the NHS (Figure 1.3). Although all three websites are directed at the general public, they are very different in content and presentational style. A quick scroll down the NHS web page shows that it is available in some European and other languages. This is clearly directed at non-English speaking users;

Figure 1.3 *NHS UK website (www.nhs.uk)*

only a few languages are listed there, which perhaps reflects the composition of the population and target users of specific language groups.

Now, let us take a look at two BBC websites: Figure 1.4 (overleaf) shows the general BBC website, and Figure 1.5 (on page 9) shows the BBC Children's website, the latter being full of images because it is aimed at children, who are likely to be more attracted to the colourful pictures of their favourite programmes and characters than to text describing the name and details of specific programmes. The general BBC site is intended for members of the general public, who are likely to be interested in news and events on different topics, to which the site provides links. As members of the public may be

Figure 1.4   *BBC website (www.bbc.co.uk)*

interested in different BBC services, the site also has links to various BBC services: radio, TV and specific news services like sports, weather and politics. These are two simple examples of two websites from the same service provider, which are quite different in their design, content and approaches because of their different sets of target customers.

Figures 1.6 and 1.7 on the following pages show the websites of two libraries: the Library of Congress (Figure 1.6) and the British Library (Figure 1.7). Although both are national libraries, a quick look at the two sites will reveal several significant differences between the two services, ranging from the look and feel of their web pages to the various search and service options.

Figure 1.5   *BBC Children website (www.bbc.co.uk/children)*

For example, the Library of Congress website has visual images and brief descriptions of several collections and links to those collections. It expects that users would be interested in any one specific collection and would therefore prefer to go directly to that collection. In contrast, although the British Library site provides brief information about some collections, like the online gallery and catalogue records, it offers two options for accessing them: a search box that appears right on top of the screen, making it the most obvious choice by users, and a browse option taking users to specific aspects of the British Library collections and services. Without further research it is not possible to make any specific comments of the merits and demerits of the two websites and their design, but one may be able to deduce that each site is driven by different approaches to design and provisions for content and services. Consequently one may conclude that a lot of user-centred research activities have been undertaken to support the design of the sites with a view

Figure 1.6 *Library of Congress website (www.loc.gov)*

to matching, as best as possible, the two national libraries' information products and services with their target customers.

Comparison of the selected web information services of different organizations shown in Figures 1.1 to 1.7 shows a number of differences in content, presentation, style and design. Many other examples of web information services may be cited that are also different in their content, approach and style. For example, the websites of any airline holiday service provide a variety of types of information, and diverse interactive features, allowing users to conduct a search for a flight, a hotel or a holiday, for example, or even to make a booking. Moving to the website of a database

Figure 1.7 *British Library website (www.bl.uk)*

search service for scholarly information, ProQuest, for example, one may find a different style of search and interaction facility, which has been designed for the potential users of the business. Thus the nature and objectives of the information service provider and the needs of its target user community, whose members use the information service, dictate the nature of the information service's design, features and facilities. A number of methods and techniques are available for assessing user requirements with a view to designing appropriate information services. Consequently, several methods and techniques are available for assessing the usability and usefulness of information services.

User studies designed to find out the information seeking and use behaviour of users is not a new area of study and certainly did not begin in the web era. Wilson (2008b) believes that the first user study in the field of information was carried out by Professor J. D. Bernal working on a preliminary analysis of a pilot questionnaire on the use of scientific literature, which was reported in the Royal Society 1948 Scientific Conference in London. He notes that regular research into the information seeking behaviour of users became common from the mid-1960s through the Aslib research group, and subsequently in the 1970s onwards by academic departments and research groups within library and information studies departments like the Centre for Research on User Studies at the University of Sheffield.

User studies

Banwell and Coulson (2004) categorized user studies into four major groups based on the focus of the study, such as:

- studies focusing on the user, which aim to investigate users' wants, needs, contexts, motivations, expectations and tasks
- studies focusing on use, which aim to investigate what one or more specific information sources are used for, and what the barriers to information access and use are
- studies focusing on the information system, which aim to investigate the characteristics of a specific information system or service with reference to its technology, design and evaluation
- studies focusing on the organization, which aim to investigate the organizational setting, management procedures and strategies including internal and external factors that have an impact on the organization.

It is not always easy to restrict a user study to one of the above categories, and most of the user studies in information studies fall into more than one of the above categories because they often have more than one focus. For example, most cases studies focus on users and information uses, or information use or user and information systems, and often information users in the context of their organization. Researchers who have attempted to study information seeking and use behaviour of people, including their individual, social and organizational characteristics, have generalized the findings, and often generated models giving a theoretical underpinning of the information behaviour of users. This is broadly called human information behaviour (HIB) research. In addition to building some new models or testing existing models, many user studies in information science have developed a methodology, and sometimes a toolkit (as in the JUBILEE project) (Banwell and Coulson, 2004).

Many user studies, especially in the context of digital libraries and online information services, have focused on information systems or services and have tried to find out how usable they are from users' and/or systems' perspectives. These studies are broadly known as usability studies, which are used to evaluate and often compare one or more information system and service; some of them have produced a benchmark or methodology that can be used by others. These are discussed in more details later in this chapter.

Human information behaviour

Wilson (2000) defined information behaviour as 'the the totality of human behaviour in relation to sources and channels of information, including both active and passive information seeking, and information use', and information seeking behaviour as 'the purposive seeking for information as a consequence of a need to satisfy some goal. In the course of seeking, the individual may interact with manual information systems (such as a newspaper or a library), or with computer-based systems (such as the World Wide Web).'

Human information behaviour as an area of research encompasses all kinds of studies in general information behaviour, information seeking and retrieval behaviour, and information use behaviour. Indeed a wide variety of research studies have been undertaken in the recent past, and many such studies have been reported in the biennial conference Information Seeking in Context (ISIC), and journals such as *Information Research, Information Processing and Management, Journal of the American Society for Information Science and Technology, Journal of Documentation* and *Journal of Information Science*. Research in different areas of HIB have been reviewed widely by several leading researchers including Ingwersen and Jarvelin (2005), Cole and Spink (2006), Foster and Spink (2007), Wilson (2008a, 2008b), Fisher and Julien (2009) and Spink (2010). Some of these works are discussed later. HIB research has moved from practice-based studies to more theory-based research. Wilson (2008b, 461) commented, 'We have seen a move, over the past 60 years, from a concern by practitioners to discover guidelines for the improvement of practice to research within an academic discipline.' Furthermore, a distinct shift in the research focus and techniques, and in the nature of the researchers may be noted. These issues are discussed later in the book.

The usability and evaluation of information services

Simply speaking, the term 'usability' means how easily a product or a service can be used. A simple dictionary definition of usability is 'the ease with which a computer interface can be efficiently and effectively used' (Reitz, 2007). This definition focuses on the ease of use of the interface of an online system or product. However, a usability study is not limited only to the study of the user interface. Kuniavsky (2003, 9) said that a usability study tells you 'whether your audience can use what you've made'. In other words, a usability study is designed to tell whether a product or service can be used easily by the target users. Thus, the notion of users and evaluation is very much integrated with usability studies. ISO 9241-11:1998 defines usability as: 'the extent to which a product can be used by specified users to achieve specified goals with effectiveness, efficiency and satisfaction in a specified context of use'. This definition tells us that in order to ascertain the usability of a product or a service we need to know:

- who the specified users are
- what their goals are in a specific context
- whether the given product or service can be used to achieve those goals.

There are three indicators to measure this: effectiveness, efficiency and satisfaction.

In the context of information science, usability studies involve user studies and the evaluation of information products and services, but user studies are much wider and do not necessarily always aim to measure the usability or performance of a given information system or service. Although often conducted in specific domains involving specific groups of users, user studies aim to investigate broader issues like the generic information behaviour of users; the impact of various socio-economic, cultural, technological, cognitive and other factors on HIB; and factors causing barriers to information access and uncertainty. Any one or more of these aspects of user studies can be used to assess the usability of a particular information product or service, but in general the overall goal of user studies or HIB research is much broader than that of a usability study, which is by definition limited to the evaluation of a specific information product or service. Wilson (1995) commented: 'Beyond the individual, and beyond the individual in interaction with the computer or the information system, however, lies the social and organizational world of the information seeker.' Research in user studies aiming to understand this began almost six decades ago and the field has moved from being merely an area of interest of some information practitioners to a field of study with a rich theory and literature behind it.

Like the field of user studies, evaluation of information systems and services also has a long history: the first formal evaluation of information retrieval systems took place in the late 1950s (Chowdhury, 2010). A quick look at the objectives of an evaluation study of an information system, as described by Lancaster (1971), showed they are similar to those of a usability study as defined by ISO 9241-11 (discussed above):

- how well the system is satisfying its objectives – the demands placed on it
- how efficiently it is satisfying its objectives
- whether the system justifies its existence.

An evaluation study can be conducted from two different points of view: from a managerial point of view the evaluation study is called management-oriented; from a user's point of view it is called a user-oriented evaluation study. Many information scientists advocate that evaluation of an information system should always be user-oriented – evaluators should pay more attention to those factors that can provide an improved service to users. Cleverdon (1978), originator of evaluation studies of information systems – methodology, metrics and so on – suggested that a user-oriented evaluation should try to answer the following questions:

- To what extent does the system meet both the expressed and latent needs of its users' community?
- What are the reasons for the failure of the system to meet users' needs?
- What is the cost-effectiveness of searches made by users themselves compared with those made by intermediaries?
- What basic changes are required to improve the output?
- Can the costs be reduced while maintaining the same level of performance?
- What would be the possible effect if some new services were introduced or an existing service were withdrawn?

Information retrieval systems have been evaluated for more than 50 years. Usability studies are of interest primarily to those involved in human–computer interaction (HCI) and the software engineering community.

They have become popular within the information community for just over a decade, especially with the introduction and proliferation of web information systems and digital libraries.

A number of models of usability have been proposed in literature. Kuniavsky (2003) suggested that there are four major steps in a usability study:

- Define users and their goals.
- Create tasks that address these goals.
- Select a group of study participants for the usability study.
- Watch them try to perform the specified tasks using the service or product whose usability is being measured.

Hearst (2009) commented that usability is an important quality of a user interface. Nielsen (2003) suggested that usability depends on five qualities of the interface of a web information service: learnability, efficiency, memorability, errors and satisfaction.

So, what's the problem?

Although specific guidelines for conducting usability studies have been developed, and various metrics have been proposed for achieving the best usability features, we still have information systems and services that are often found to be difficult to use, or those that do not always produce the best result or output expected by users. Hearst (2009, 5) observed that 'despite the newly recognized importance of usability and user interface design, it is nonetheless surprisingly difficult to design highly usable interfaces'.

There are several reasons for this, which may be grouped broadly into two categories: purpose-related and resource-related. An information service or product may be designed for a different purpose – in some cases it may be designed to provide a service or a product that is free at the point of use, for example the Europeana Digital Library (Figure 1.8), which enables people to explore the digital resources of Europe's museums, libraries, archives and audiovisual collections, or it may be designed to sell a specific item or a product, for example, Amazon's Kindle. No matter how ingenious and innovative the designers may be, they are always constrained by the resources required to develop a product or service. In other words, despite their best efforts and wishes, designers often have to make compromises over the features and facilities offered in an information product or a service.

Figure 1.8   *The Europeana Digital Library home page (www.europeana.eu)*

Other factors are becoming increasingly difficult to meet in the internet age, because users of an information service or product like Europeana can be anyone anywhere with specific language and information skills, a specific education and cultural background influencing their information needs and expectations, and different levels of ICT equipment and facilities, and yet the product or service designers have to aim to meet every user's information need, and design a service that ideally allows everyone to find the required information effectively, efficiently and with a high level of satisfaction (as stated in the International Organization for Standardization definition of usability discussed earlier in this chapter).

A closer look at some web-based information services of university libraries quickly shows that they have significant differences on several accounts. Figures 1.9 to 1.12 on the following pages show the first screen of the library web pages of four universities, including two that are among the leading academic institutions in the world. A quick look at their first screens shows some significant differences in content, approach and layout. The UTS Library web page provides a lot of information, and includes a search box that allows users to look for books, journals or databases directly from that web page, whereas although the first page of the University of Strathclyde

Library takes users directly to the page that allows them to search for an item, among other options, one cannot conduct a catalogue search before passing through two further screens. Without making any specific comments about the efficiency of any particular library's web-based library and information service, one can observe that the two examples discussed here would score differently if judged against usability criteria.

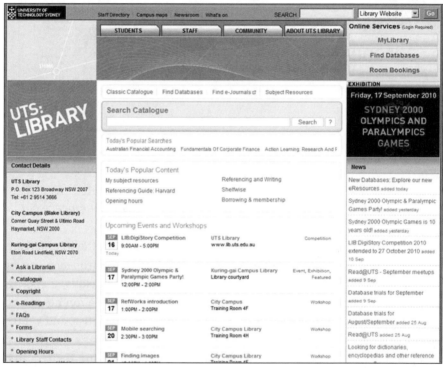

Figure 1.9 *The UTS Library home page (www.lib.uts.edu.au/)*

Figure 1.10 *The University of Strathclyde Library home page (www.lib.strath.ac.uk/)*

Similar differences can also be found between the websites of the libraries of the world's top universities. For example, a quick look at Figure 1.11 shows that the first page of the University of Oxford's web page on libraries provides information about the University's libraries and their various services, but a user has to go though a number of screens before being able to carry out a simple search on one of the libraries' catalogues. The home page of MIT Libraries (Figure 1.12 overleaf), on the other hand, while giving links to the key services available, also provides a simple search facility on the same page. Again, without comparing and commenting on their specific merits and demerits, the usability of the two information services clearly varies.

Figure 1.11 *The University of Oxford web page on libraries (www.ox.ac.uk/)*

Similar differences may be noted in the web pages of specific online information services providers like ProQuest and Factiva or information products and services like the ISI Web of Knowledge and JSTOR. These examples show that there are significant differences in specific information

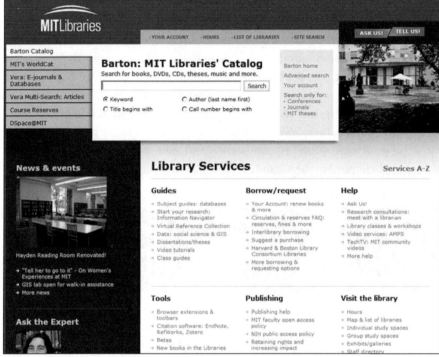

Figure 1.12   *MIT Libraries web page (http://libraries.mit.edu/)*

products and services. Scores of similar examples may be drawn from online service providers, library websites, digital libraries and so on showing that variations in style, approach, content, retrieval and access facilities exist. As a result the usability of these information products and services varies, and clearly it is neither possible nor necessary for every information product and service to have the same usability features. Often the diversity is necessary for several reasons, and adds character and value to any information service or product. However, information professionals – whether designers or service providers – should always be mindful of usability and evaluation techniques so they can assess the qualities and appropriateness of an information product or service. This is the justification for this book.

About this book

The introductory discussions in this chapter have demonstrated that in order to design and develop a good information service or product it is necessary to study the characteristics, goals and information behaviour of potential users, to enable them to achieve their goal effectively and efficiently. Usable systems do not emerge by accident; they are the outcome of a series of carefully designed research and development activities arising from a relatively new area of study in the computer and software world called usability engineering (Leventhal and Barnes, 2008).

Usability studies have become common in the context of information products and services over the past few years. There are three common themes in any information product or service:

- There is one or more user.
- The user is doing something for which they need information.
- The information service or product is designed to enable the user to accomplish the goal by obtaining the necessary information easily.

In addition, it is necessary to consider the overall user experience by looking at users' entire interaction with the information product or service, and the thoughts, feelings, perceptions and enrichment that result from it (Tullis and Albert, 2008). Until fairly recently expensive and time-consuming studies had to be conducted in order to gather data on the overall user experience. Nowadays modern web technologies and various research methods and tools enable us to conduct online usability testing involving a large number of local and/or remote users. By combining appropriate methods and techniques it is possible to gather various usability information from users: what they like and don't like, which part of the information product or service they use more than others, and for what reasons, what possible measures may be taken to improve a product or service, and so on. Albert, Tullis and Tedesco (2010) suggested that usability testing provides answers to questions like:

- Is there a difference between alternative designs of a product or service?
- What design characteristics do users like (and what don't they like)?
- How significant are the different usability issues?
- Where are users likely to abandon a transaction and why?
- How do various users – individuals and/or groups – interact with the design and the product or service?

Thus, online usability testing gives us a valuable insight into the overall user experience, which may be immensely valuable in improving and/or tailoring an information product or service. It is imperative that information practitioners and researchers who are engaged in designing new information products and services, or assessing the usability of existing information services or products, have a good background in user studies and usability testing.

This book aims to address information users and the usability of information products and services from the perspectives of information professionals. By drawing examples from several past and ongoing research and development activities, and pointing out various tools, techniques and standards used to understand the nature and characteristics of users from the perspectives of different types of information services, it prepares information professionals facing different challenges of meeting user needs and expectations in the rapidly changing digital information world.

The book has ten chapters. The first chapter provides a basic introduction to the subject and thus presents an outline of the book. Chapter 2 discusses the concept of information users, and briefly discusses different research methods for conducting user studies. Chapter 3 discusses the basics of HIB and briefly discusses some important HIB models. Human information behaviour is a huge area of research; and hundreds of books and thousands of research papers have been written addressing different areas of HIB. Therefore this chapter is not exhaustive; its aim is to provide readers with a quick introduction to various HIB models and some studies so they can relate them to the usability of information products and services.

Chapter 4 discusses the concept of usability and various usability models and study techniques. Although usability forms a major part of HCI in general, and user interfaces in particular, the discussions in this chapter focus on the usability of different types of information products and services. Chapters 5 and 6 discuss different aspects of usability studies in the context of web information services and digital libraries. The discussions are supported by illustrations showing different types of usability and evaluation studies of web information services and digital libraries.

The next two chapters take a broader view of usability and focus on the overall user experience in the digital information age, which is influenced by a variety of socio-economic and technological features. Chapter 7 discusses the issues of accessibility and different barriers to digital information access that influence the usability and impact of digital information services on different sections of our society. Chapter 8 discusses a few selected case studies of evaluation and usability studies that had different study objectives and methods, and produced different results. This will give readers an idea of how usability and evaluation studies vary in design, research methods and findings, and how critical decisions need to be made depending on the nature and objectives of different studies. Chapter 9 discusses the digital divide and social inclusion in the context of digital information products and services. It provides a European and global perspective of the digital divide and its impact on digital information services. Chapter 10 closes the book with a discussion of the current research and trends in the context of usability and evaluation of digital information services.

Summary

Users have always been at the centre of library and information services, and user studies have remained a major area of research within information science for over five decades. Usability studies that appeared as part of HCI and software engineering research have become popular within the information science community over the past decade. A variety of usability methods and techniques have been developed to assess the effectiveness, efficiency and suitability of a variety of web-based information services and digital libraries. Within the context of modern information products and services, this book discusses different methods, techniques and research related to users and usability in the digital age. It also discusses the major barriers to the success of digital information services with special reference to the digital divide, and provides a snapshot of the trends in information users and usability research.

References

Albert, B., Tullis, T. and Tedesco, D. (2010) *Beyond the Usability Lab: conducting large-scale online user experience studies*, Morgan Kaufmann.

Banwell, L. and Coulson, G. (2004) Users and User Study Methodology: the JUBILEE project, *Information Research*, **9** (2).

Chowdhury, G. G. (2010) *Introduction to Modern Information Retrieval*, 3rd edn, Facet Publishing.

Cleverdon, C. W. (1978) User Evaluation of Information Retrieval Systems. In King, D. W. (ed.), *Key Papers in Design and Evaluation of Retrieval Systems*, Knowledge Industry, 154–65.

Cole, C. and Spink, A. (2006) *New Directions in Human Information Behaviour*, Springer.

Cutter, C. A. (1904) *Rules for a Dictionary Catalog*, 4th edn, Government Printing

Office.

Fisher, K. and Julien, H. (2009) Information Behavior, *Annual Review of Information Science and Technology*, **43**, 317–58.

Foster, A. and Spink, A. (eds) (2007) Human Information Behaviour, *Journal of Documentation*, **63** (1), special issue, 166.

Hearst, M. (2009) *Search User Interfaces*, Cambridge University Press.

Ingwersen, P. and Jarvelin, K. (2005) *The Turn: integration of information seeking and retrieval in context*, Springer.

ISO 9241-11:1998 *Ergonomic Requirements for Office Work with Visual Display Terminals (VDTs); part II: guidance on usability*, International Organization for Standardization, www.iso.org/iso/catalogue_detail.htm?csnumber=16883.

Kuniavsky, M. (2003) *Observing the User Experience: a practitioner's guide to user research*, Morgan Kaufmann.

Lancaster, F. W. (1971) The Cost-Effectiveness Analysis of Information Retrieval and Dissemination Systems, *Journal of the American Society for Information Science*, **22** (1), 12–27.

Leventhal, L. and Barnes, J. (2008) *Usability Engineering: process, products and examples*, Pearson/Prentice Hall.

Nielsen, J. (2003) *Usability 101: introduction to usability*, www.useit.com/alertbox/20030825.html.

Ranganathan, S. R. (1963) *The Five Laws of Library Science*, 2nd edn, Asia Publishing House.

Reitz, J. M. (2007) *ODLIS: Online Dictionary for Library and Information Science*, Libraries Unlimited, http://lu.com/odlis/.

Spink, A. (2010) *Information Behaviour: an evolutionary instinct*, Springer-Verlag.

Svenonius. E. (2001) *The Intellectual Foundation of Information Organization*, 2nd edn, MIT Press.

Tullis, T. and Albert, B. (2008) *Measuring the User Experience: collecting, analyzing, and presenting usability metrics*, Morgan Kaufmann.

Wilson, T. (1995) Modelling the Information User: the wider perspective, paper delivered at the INFOTECH '95 Conference, Kuala Lumpur, Malaysia, November 1995, http://informationr.net/tdw/publ/papers/klpaper.html.

Wilson, T. (2000) Human Information Behaviour: informing science, *Information Science Research*, special issue, **3** (2).

Wilson, T. (2008a) The Information User: past, present and future, *Journal of Information Science*, **34** (4), 457–64.

Wilson, T. D. (2008b) On User Studies and Information Needs, *Journal of Documentation*, special issue, 174–86.

2

Information needs and user studies

Introduction

Wilson (2000) commented, 'However we define it, and from whatever year we choose to date it, information science has been concerned with the information user.' As discussed in Chapter 1, user studies, as we understand them today, first appeared as an area of research in the context of information studies in 1948. Over the past six decades user studies has remained a major area of research, giving rise to several theories, models and new principles published in thousands of research papers and reports. Later Wilson (2008, 174) observed that 'apart from information retrieval theories virtually no other area of information science . . . has occasioned as much research effort and writing as "user studies"'.

In October 2010 a quick search on the ISI Web of Knowledge database for 'user studies' produced 11,798 hits: 6534 hits in computer science, 2848 in engineering, 2279 in psychology, 2268 in education and educational research, 1702 in behavioural sciences, 1298 in telecommunications, 1265 in information and library science, and 1042 in health sciences, demonstrating that user studies is a major area of research in different disciplines. Wilson (2008) observed that 'information needs' has remained a major area of investigation within user studies but, commenting on this claim, Bawden (2008) pointed out that progress towards having a theoretical understanding of information needs has been slow.

User studies and information needs are increasingly challenging areas of research in the modern digital age, where numerous information products are services are being created for consumption by remote and widely varied categories of users. Some typical examples of information in a variety of information products and services were discussed in Chapter 1; for example the two BBC websites shown in Figures 1.4 and 1.5 show examples of different kinds of information services designed for different categories of customers of the BBC. Illustrations of other websites in Chapter 1 demonstrated that every organization or institution takes a different approach in designing and offering their online information products and services in order to meet the needs of their target audience or customers. Other examples of information products and services range from numerous search engines and digital libraries to handheld communication and entertainment devices such as mobile phones, iPods and iPads, and e-books readers like the Sony e-book readers and Amazon Kindle. Therefore 'understanding the consumer data, information and knowledge, is becoming increasingly important in relation to the design and development of electronic information products and services' (Hepworth, 2007). Consequently, a variety of methods and techniques have been developed by researchers to study users and their information behaviour in a variety of contexts and domains. Although, modern-day user studies for different products and services are conducted within various disciplines and professions, they have their origin in information science. This chapter provides an introduction to some of the techniques and methods used to gather information about users, and their information needs and information behaviour.

Information needs

Although it has been a major theme of research in information science for several decades, the term 'information need' is often difficult to define, study, quantify or measure. Information need is often a result of some unresolved problem(s). It may arise when individuals recognize that their current state of knowledge is insufficient to cope with the task in hand, to resolve conflicts in a subject area, or to fill a void in some area of knowledge. However, an information need is not a primary need, but a secondary need that arises out of another need. Nicholas and Herman (2009) observed that when people experience a problem or a difficulty, or when they are under some pressure – for example when they are required to perform a task, solve a problem, go somewhere or purchase an item – their cognitive and emotional needs may be fully or partially met by obtaining and using information. People's information needs can be aligned with Maslow's hierarchy of needs (see Maslow, 1954), and thus five kinds of information needs can be identified:

- *The need for coping information*: The information needs of people at the lowest level for coping with a stress, job or task.
- *The need for helping information*: The information needed to avoid risk and danger in everyday jobs, activities and decision making. This may come from a variety of background information resources such as subject or discipline-based references, tools, standards, practices and so on that enlighten people and make them more suitable or better equipped with performing their daily activities and handling problems.
- *The need for enlightening information*: The information needed by people when they are higher up in Maslow's need hierarchy. It provides insights, enlightens people about certain activities, and allows them to understand why people do what they do – the broader business and social implications of various actions. This information may come from documentary and human expert sources – meetings, networks and so on.
- *The need for empowering information*: The information needed by people when they are higher up Maslow's need hierarchy and aim to achieve esteem. This information is different from that required for day-to-day activities or background information. It is required to get a better understanding of the business environment and context, and can be obtained by understanding company or business information policies and strategies, and political or economic information related to the environment and context. The information sources may be formal or informal and can be more expert-based than document-based.
- *The need for edifying information*: The information required by those who have reached the highest level of Maslow's hierarchy, who need information for self-actualization and self-fulfilment. This information may be related not to handling a specific job or resolving a specific problem, but instead to a much higher level of psychological attainment. Such inform-ation may be obtained from information resources on religion, psychology, history, science and so on, or from human experts – mentors and gurus.

Before identifying the challenges associated with the study of information need, it is important to distinguish three terms often mistakenly used to describe the same thing while in reality they are completely different: information need, information want and information demand. While we have already noted that an 'information need' is a secondary need that arises when people want to perform a task, face a challenge or problem, fulfil a curiosity, or acquire some level of satisfaction or accomplishment, 'information want' denotes what people think they need or would like to have, and therefore could be a wish list that depends on a number of factors, such as the person's background and surroundings, their familiarity with the product, and the product's affordability. Clearly, therefore, a gap exists between the information need and information want of a person. Similarly 'information demand' may or may not be the same as the information need and information want: an information demand is a request for information that is believed to be wanted.

To put these terms in the perspective of food, one may say that 'information need' is like the need for good quality and healthy food; 'information want' is like a person's wish list, for example a desire for Chinese or Mexican food; and 'information demand' is like the order placed after reading a menu. Sometimes we realize that the food we ordered was not what we wanted and more importantly not what we needed. How many times have we wished that we had ordered the dish that the person on the next table is having! This situation occurs commonly in the information world – often we may not realize exactly what information we need to better perform a task or solve a problem, so what we want and finally demand may not necessarily be most appropriate for our true information need.

Several challenges are associated with the study of information need:

- Information need is a relative concept. It depends on several factors and does not remain constant: it changes in accordance with institutional or personal context, and is greatly influenced by social context and external (political, economic) factors.
- Information needs change over a period of time.
- Information needs vary from person to person, from job to job, subject to subject, organization to organization, and so on.
- People's information needs are largely dependent on the environment. For example, the information needs of those in an academic environment are different from those in an industrial, business or government/administrative environment.
- Measuring (quantifying) information need is difficult.
- Information need often remains unexpressed or poorly expressed because most information services expect their users to formulate a query on something that they do not know, or are not an expert on, in the first place. Consequently, in most cases, people fail to choose the most appropriate terms or expression to submit to the search system, and as a

result the search output is not always quite as good as it should be.
- Information need often changes on receipt of some information. Sometimes, after obtaining a piece of information people may feel that they need another piece of information to decipher or to make use of it; in other cases, they may feel that the retrieved information was not the one that they were looking for, or they may need some more information to get a better understanding or make the most appropriate use of it.

Taylor (1991) identified four major types of information need in the context of a library search that lead the user from the state of a purely conceptual need to a formally expressed and then constrained (by the environment) need:

Visceral need → Conscious need → Formalized need → Compromised need

Where:

- The visceral need is the unconscious need.
- The conscious need is conscious but undefined.
- The formalized need is formally expressed need.
- The compromised need is an expressed need influenced by internal and external constraints such as the cost of information, language difficulties, time lag or delays in obtaining the information.

Xie (2008) suggests that Taylor's work has formed the foundation of several research studies in interactive information seeking and retrieval including those of Belkin (1980), Kuhlthau (2004) and Ingwersen (1996), which are discussed later in this book (Chapter 3). Wilson in his 1981 model of user studies provided a schematic view of what people do when they have an information need. He subsequently modified and extended this model to show how information needs trigger information seeking and how this is influenced by several contextual – social, cultural and so on – factors. Wilson's 1981 model is discussed in the next section, and his modified model is discussed later in this book.

Analysis of information needs

As Nicholas and Herman (2009) observed, most information systems seldom undertake regular consumer evaluation with special reference to user needs or usage data. There are several reasons for this:

- Information systems professionals often do not feel it necessary to consult users on professional matters; they assume they already have the necessary expertise, and that people would not understand their complex skills and training.
- Information services are dominated by systems-centred rather than user-centred approaches, so information systems specialists make the most of design decisions without appropriate inputs from users. In many institutions, library and information professionals do not have the opportunity to communicate with their customers because of resource constraints, the institutional hierarchy or other such reasons. This acts as a hindrance to building close customer relationships.
- Gathering and analysing data on users' information needs is not an easy task.
- Gathering information needs data is resource intensive and it is often difficult to justify the required resources when information services constantly face a severe budget crisis.
- There is a lack of a commonly understood and standard framework assessment of information needs. This does not mean that there are no standards or frameworks – as discussed in the following sections and later in this book, many models and standards have been developed by information researchers – but there is hardly any framework or standard that is commonly accepted and can be used by anyone under any circumstances.

Nicholas and Herman (2009) proposed an 11-point framework for analysis of information need, which is discussed with the other approaches to the study of information need in the section 'Factors affecting information needs' (page 34).

User studies

Hjørland (2000) defined user studies as 'investigations of the use and users (including non-users and potential uses and users) of documents, information, communication channels, information systems and information services'. This definition of user studies is significant in a number of ways. First, it reminds us that user studies can be conducted in the context of information products, services, systems or channels of information access and/or delivery – aggregators, search engines and so on. Second, user studies should be limited to users of an information product, service or channel, but should include potential users and even non-users, as we want to know why people do not use the information product or service, and how to reach this potential user community.

Despite the difficulties of resources and logistics associated with the practical aspects of conducting large-scale user needs analysis studies, researchers have long been engaged in developing methods and techniques for conducting user studies of different kinds. In his well known and widely cited paper, Wilson (1981) presented a schematic view of different aspects of user studies in the context of information science (Figure 2.1). This model has been studied, reviewed, discussed and debated in over 100 top ranking journal and conference papers. According to this model, a user may turn to formal information systems like a library or database of scholarly information, or can turn to other personal or institutional information sources like estate agents.

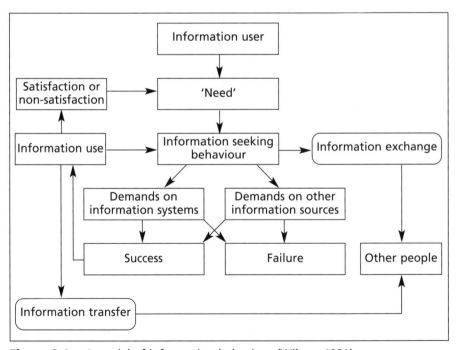

Figure 2.1   *A model of information behaviour (Wilson, 1981)*

Although Wilson proposed his first information behaviour model (Wilson, 1981) almost three decades ago, and several major changes have taken place in information studies since then, especially with the introduction of the web and proliferation of web-based information services and products, it still holds good today. According to this model, people with an information need approach either conventional information systems – libraries, databases and so on – or other human or institutional sources such as estate agents, as Wilson (1981) suggested, and this process continues until they find what they are looking for or decide to stop looking for the information. While this generic approach still holds good, in today's web environment, most information transactions take place through the web – whether on typical library and information databases, digital libraries and so on, or general databases for information available in a myriad of institutional and personal information resources as well as social networks and shared information spaces.

A modified version of Wilson's model in today's context is presented in Figure 2.2. A user today, when engaged in a specific task or activity within a given context (an important concept in information behaviour studies, as discussed later in this book), feels an information need, which then prompts them to engage in an information seeking activity. Most interactions take place through the web and social networks. The user goes to the web – either the web in general, through a search engine or specific information service accessible through the web or a social network group like Facebook, or a shared service like YouTube.

This is very different from the conventional approach discussed in Wilson's original model. The web has become the major information channel that people use for accessing different kinds of information resources, be they typical libraries and scholarly databases, digital libraries, institutional and individual web pages, or social networks. So, the options 'other information sources' as mentioned in Wilson's model (Figure 2.1) are now endless. They include virtually every bit of information available on the web from personal and institutional web pages, blogs, wikis, commercial and open source and shared information sources, and social networks. Similarly people use social networks for connecting to 'other people' (in Wilson's model, Figure 2.1), and different kinds of shared information interactions and interchange, for example through Facebook groups or wikis, take place there. Sometimes people choose to use a specific type of information channel like library and scholarly databases, social networks or the web, but increasingly search

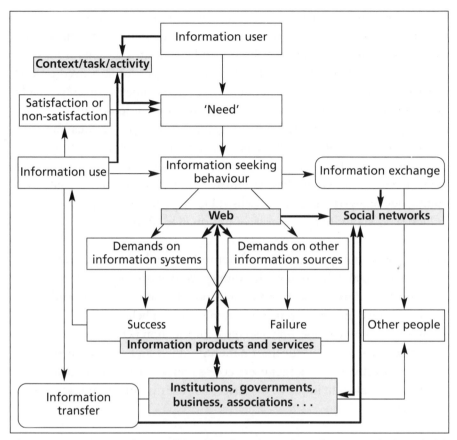

Figure 2.2 *User studies model in the digital age (text, boxes and links in bold have been added to show the changes)*

engines are becoming the first port of call for information searching that retrieves information from all of these channels. Therefore users may obtain a required piece of information from a scholarly information source, an institutional or individual web page, a blog, a social network like Facebook, or a video sharing site like YouTube.

One major change to information needs and information users has been brought by the web that was not possible, or at least not easily achievable, in the traditional information behaviour model, and hence is not evident in Wilson's model (Figure 2.1): the addition of the information needs of creators and producers. The web now enables companies, businesses and institutions engaged in developing information products and services to gather various information about their customers, directly or indirectly, in order to make their information products and services more suitable for the market and users. For instance, information about user behaviour is gleaned from social networks and fed into decision making and strategies for improved product and service design. Thus the modern web environment not only enables users of information products and services to find their information, but also allows producers of information to gather and glean various pieces of information about their customers. Thus two-way information use and interaction now take place. Some of these are obvious and take place in real time; others are carried out through further analysis of transaction data (data mining, log analysis and so on, discussed later in this chapter).

Figure 2.2 shows two categories of information users:

- users for whom specific information products and services are designed and developed, who interact through specific information systems or channels, and use those information products and services depending on their context, information needs and information behaviour
- information producers, who also have information needs, for example to find out how their specific information products and services meet their stated objectives, how target users access and use them, what measures need to be taken to improve the success of their products and services, and so on.

A variety of methods and techniques are used to study users and their information behaviour in general or in specific environments in relation to specific institutions, domains or contexts, and in relation to specific information products and services. Some of these methods and techniques are discussed briefly in this chapter, and some are discussed in relation to specific users and usability studies later in the book.

Factors affecting information needs

Wilson later expanded his 1981 model (Wilson, 1999) to show various factors that influence users' information needs and information-seeking behaviour. In his revised model Wilson pointed out that information needs are secondary needs, caused by primary needs arising from a problem or a task on hand, and therefore a particular information need is influenced 'by the context, which can be the person him or herself, or the role the person plays in work and life, or the environments (social, political, economical, technological and so on), which in accordance with definitions in psychology can be defined as physiological, cognitive or affective' (Niedźwiedzka, 2003). Figure 2.3 shows Wilson's model where he used the term 'intervening variables' – they are not necessarily obstacles but variables, and their impact may be supportive of information use as well as preventive.

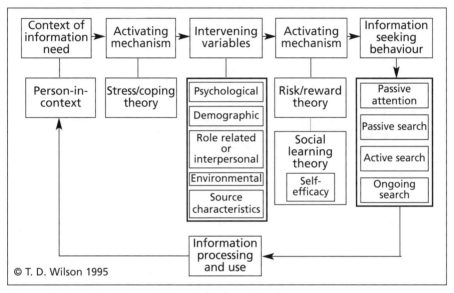

Figure 2.3 *Wilson's model (1996) (Wilson, 1999)*

While the intervening variables identified by Wilson over two decades ago still hold good, many researchers have added new variables that affect users' information needs, access and use in today's digital age. In 1996 Saracevic proposed his stratified model of information retrieval interactions (Figure 2.4 overleaf), which shows the interactions taking place between a user and a computer system through an interface in the context of information retrieval. Users interact with an information retrieval system through a query, and receive responses from the system. Computers process the content and use the hardware and software systems to facilitate user interactions with the information retrieval system. On the user side the process is physical and cognitive, involving query formulation (and query modifications, if necessary); visualization, understanding (with reference to context), selection and/or rejection of the retrieved items; and repetition of the entire process until a decision is made to stop, either on receipt of the required information

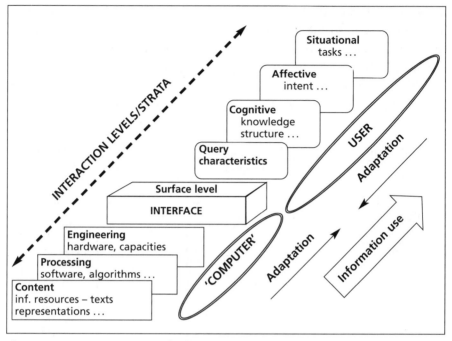

Figure 2.4   *Saracevic's stratified model of IT interaction (Saracevic, 1997)*

or for any other reason. A number of researchers have attempted to understand and model the interactions and cognitive processes that take place when users retrieve information. Detailed discussion of these models is beyond the scope of this book, but an understanding of human information behaviour (HIB) research, which aims to understand and model user interactions with digital information systems, is essential for developing usable information products and services. Some of these studies and models are discussed in Chapter 3.

Based on their experience of conducting user studies for about two decades, Nicholas and Herman (2009) identified 11 major characteristics of information needs, which can be used as a framework for evaluation of information needs: subject, function, nature, intellectual level, viewpoint, quantity, quality or authority, date or currency, place of publication or origin, processing and packaging. These characteristics of information needs are determined and often influenced by the user and the context. For example, the subject characteristics of an information need may range from the simple, arising from a specific subject like the chemical formula of water, to the complex, involving a variety of disciplines and subjects, such as the operation of space shuttles or the impact of industrialization on climate change. Similarly the function, intended use, nature and characteristics of the information depend on the user, their role and context, and some characteristics are attributes of the information required by the user such as quantity, authority, currency, origin and packaging. Again, these are closely related to the nature and function of the user. For example, in some professions users need the most current information available; in others, users need comprehensive historical information. A city trader or someone looking for the best mortgage deals needs the most up-to-date information, which can change daily; someone looking for a typical council service like a special uplift request (of an unwanted waste item) or how to apply for permission to build an extension needs information that is relatively static.

In addition, users' information needs and consequently user studies in today's digital world depend significantly on users' access to, and use of, ICT in general and the internet in particular. All the intervening variables identified in Wilson's model (Figure 2.3) and all the information characteristics identified by Nicholas and Herman (discussed above) can be significantly influenced by the digital characteristics of the user – whether a digital native or a digital migrant. Digital natives, sometimes called the Google generation, are people who have grown up in the internet era and have typical characteristics relating to their access and use of digital information. Their first port of call when looking for information is a web or social network; they use internet and mobile technologies for almost every information-related activity, and are not used to spending too much time on searching for information. See Gunter, Rowlands and Nicholas (2009) and Rowlands et al. (2008). These characteristics are different from those of digital migrants, who have adopted, and to some extent adapted, digital technologies in their day-to-day activities. Figure 2.2 shows the key role played by the web and social networks in today's digital information landscape and how together they shape, influence and play a critical role in users' information needs and information behaviour. Web and social networking technologies are used extensively by consumer and information creator and producer groups, which aim to make the best use of these powerful technologies to influence and benefit from each other. Some of them are discussed in subsequent chapters in this book.

User study methods

Early user studies focused on scientific research methods that employed a positivist or reductionist approach. Researchers were driven by working through stages such as problem definition, classification of phenomena, hypothesis formulation, data collection, hypothesis testing and so forth, and the interaction of theory and method, with the large-scale social survey as the predominant method of data collection. This resulted in quantitative analysis and interpretation of data (Wilson, 2000). More recent researchers carrying out user studies are increasingly adopting interpretive approaches that attempt to explain observations without making some of the assumptions or hypotheses based on some preconceived ideas on which the scientific method is based. These are discussed below in the context of quantitative and qualitative approaches to research.

Commenting on earlier user studies, Wilson (2000) noted that 'the practitioners of information work have been disappointed by user-studies research, largely because they fail to find within it recommendations for service provision. Equally, information researchers have generally failed to make an impact within any social scientific discipline because their work lacks integration with theories within those disciplines.' In other words, earlier user studies, which are largely based on quantitative approaches, did not depict the details of the context within which the information access and use phenomena take place, and therefore often failed to paint a picture of what happens on the ground and why. Arguing in favour of a qualitative approach to research that is more firmly based on social science research principles, Wilson (2000) suggested that 'the answer to the first of these problems may lie in turning to a different model of research, where its application or utilization is considered to be part of the process'. He proposed that 'qualitative research' is a way of confronting directly the issue of the lack of theory in user studies.

Qualitative vs quantitative research in user studies

As discussed in the previous section, researchers carrying out early user studies adopted quantitative approaches that aimed to generate data on specific phenomenon thereby telling us what is happening in a given instance. Qualitative research on the other hand 'draws data from the context in which events occur, in an attempt to describe these occurrences, as a means of determining the process in which events are embedded and the perspectives of those participating in the events, using induction to derive possible explanations based on observed phenomenon' (Gorman and Clayton, 2005, 3). Qualitative research aims to understand users and their various characteristics and so on from their perspectives. Thus while the quantitative approach to user studies lies within the positivist paradigm, the qualitative approach lies within the interpretivist paradigm. Gorman and Clayton (2005) provided a comparison of the quantitative and qualitative approaches, which has been reproduced in Table 2.1.

Table 2.1 shows that quantitative research aims to generate facts and figures related to an event or issue based on some predefined hypothesis and formal instruments; qualitative research aims to generate a theory as it progresses, and it requires the personal involvement of the researcher within the event or the process being studied. While quantitative research employs a variety of methods for generating quantitative data, which can be analysed to generate statistically proven findings and conclusions, qualitative approaches aim to understand a phenomenon and build a theory based on it. Thus while quantitative researchers employ experimental or survey methods to generate numeric data, qualitative researchers carrying out user studies often employ:

Table 2.1 Differences between qualitative and quantitative research		
Characteristics	Qualitative research	Quantitative research
Assumptions	Social construction of reality Primacy of subject matter Complexity of variables Difficulty in measuring variables	Objective reality of social facts Primacy of method Possible to identify variables Possible to measure variables
Purpose	Contextualization Interpretation Understanding participant perspectives	Generalization Prediction Causal explanation
Approach	Theory generating Emergence and portrayal Researcher as instrument Naturalistic Inductive Pattern seeking Looking for pluralism and complexity Descriptive	Hypothesis based Manipulation and control Uses formal instruments Experimentation Deductive Component analysis Seeking norms and consensus Reducing data to numerical indices
Researcher's role	Personal involvement and partiality Empathetic understanding	Detachment and impartiality Objective portrayal

- ethnography, normally used in sociology and anthropology, combining interviews and observations
- action research where the observer or interviewer takes on the role of a subject by participating in the activity under study and observing the phenomenon under study more closely, often through the eyes of the actual user or participant
- case studies where one or more specific cases are chosen to study certain issues intensively and critically.

The qualitative approach is neither superior nor inferior to the quantitative approach and sometimes both approaches and multiple strategies need to be adopted in user studies, to allow the researcher to use a range of methods and data collection instruments. Gorman and Clayton (2005, 13) observed that by employing methods from quantitative and qualitative studies, and positivist and interpretive paradigms, the researcher can compensate for inherent weaknesses in each approach. They further suggested that 'by using a quantitative method in conjunction with a qualitative method, the researcher is able to draw on the unique strengths of each – thus providing both macro- and micro-level perspectives in a single project'.

Methods of data collection

A variety of data collections methods are employed in user studies; the most common user-centred methods are questionnaire, interview, focus group, observation and diary. There are also various software-based techniques like interaction-tracking, eye-tracking and transaction log analysis.

Questionnaires

Questionnaires are the most popular instruments for user studies. They can be extremely flexible and helpful to gather information from large or small numbers of users on any topic. However, the task of designing an appropriate questionnaire is not easy and requires a lot of time and skill. It is useful to have a pilot run of the questionnaire among a small subset of users before the final version is distributed. This helps improve the questionnaire by modifying, adding or deleting some of the questions, avoiding redundancy, and so on.

A questionnaire may comprise closed or open questions. Closed questions allow the respondent to answer by choosing between alternatives provided by the researcher: 'yes' or 'no'. The advantage of this type of question is that the data can be easily collected and analysed and questions can be easily answered by respondents. Through a closed question the researcher can direct the respondent to choose one of many specified responses. The disadvantage of closed questions is that respondents might:

- have to choose more than one option to provide the correct answer
- not always find an appropriate choice from the available alternatives
- need to be subjective in their reply to certain questions, which they might not feel comfortable with.

Sometimes shades of opinion are asked for, in which case respondents may be asked to respond using a sliding scale.

Open questions require respondents to formulate the answer in their own words. This is a more undirected approach, giving more freedom to respondents. It is an effective technique when respondents are expected to express their answer or opinion succinctly in written form. Analysis of responses to such questions is likely to be more complex and thus time-consuming because answers often comprise long sentences, possibly in a different language from that of the analyser, and one that may involve jargon or be based on particular assumptions or prior knowledge. In some cases, a combination of open and closed questions may be helpful.

These are the major advantages of the questionnaire method in user studies:

- It is cheap and flexible.
- Respondents can be anonymous.
- Questions can be presented in a consistent format and style.
- It is an impersonal method of research; information can be provided anonymously by the participant and the method is not obtrusive (the researcher does not get to know or see the respondent).
- The survey work can be completed at the respondent's own pace and convenience.

The disadvantages of this method are:

- It may lead to a lack of qualitative depth because often respondents do not get enough scope (or even space) to give a detailed response to a specific issue.
- Once the questions have been formulated, they cannot be modified appropriately to the answers received, as is possible in some other survey methods.
- Answers can be given only to the questions that are asked (no new question can be added to follow up an answer, as is possible in some other methods such as interviews).
- Answers may be inaccurate, incomplete or distorted.

Questionnaires may be helpful for user studies when:

- dealing with a large number of users required for generating numerical and statistical data
- relatively straightforward information is required and the responses can be coded easily and numerically for analysis and interpretation
- the research topic and environment is conducive for respondents to provide open and honest responses
- anonymity is an important factor or an essential requirement of research
- numerical data is expected or straightforward opinion or comments are wanted
- a large number of respondents can be reached easily
- the researcher is sure respondents will understand the questions and what is expected of them
- other data collection methods are not suitable for reasons of resources, accessibility to the respondents and so on
- an unobtrusive method is preferred
- a researcher wants to gather data from a large number of people in one go.

These are some basic guidelines that may help a researcher conduct user studies through questionnaires:

- Keep the questionnaire short and simple.
- Try to put the questions in a logical order.

- Use simple words and plain and easy to understand language.
- Keep sentences short, and avoid ambiguity.
- Use a clear type face that is easy to read and understand.
- Pay attention to the layout and design.
- Decide what exactly it is you want to know, formulate the question, then ask yourself whether you would give an answer to the question that would be appropriate for the research; modify, if necessary.

Interviews

Interviews are one of the most commonly employed methods of data collection in qualitative research. An interview involves asking set questions to a selected group of respondents. They are often employed in user studies as a method for collecting qualitative data. They are similar to questionnaires in that respondents are asked specific questions, but they are conducted in person with a single respondent, with provisions for guiding that person towards a specific research goal or asking instant follow-up questions based on responses obtained. The interview method is a useful means of surveying a representative population sample covering all shades of opinion. The questions asked provide opportunities for qualified answers, and the interviewer may prompt the respondent if necessary.

An interview may be structured or semi-structured. A structured interview is like an oral questionnaire. Structured interviews help the researcher keep control over the process of the interview, and the responses obtained are easy to analyse and consolidate. Semi-structured interviews provide more scope for discussion and recording the respondent's opinions and views. The interview schedule should be carefully designed and consist of a number of fairly specific questions, each of which may be expanded.

Interviews are often recorded and the interviewer may take notes. They are powerful instruments for collecting data because each interview gives the interviewer an opportunity to get a better insight into what is happening and why. Sometimes interviews are used as a triangulation method, jointly in combination with other methods of data collection such as questionnaires, for verifying or probing specific issues or points identified through other data collection instruments such as questionnaires. Gorman and Clayton (2005) identified the following advantages of interviews as a method of data collection:

- *Immediacy*: Data can be obtained immediately in response to a question.
- *Mutual exploration*: The interviewer and the respondent can create an environment of mutual exploration of certain issues.
- *Investigation of causation*: Interviews allow a researcher to find out the cause of some incidents through discussions and exploration.
- *Personal contact*: Interviews allow the researcher to establish personal contact with the respondents, which may be helpful for data collection.
- *Speed*: Interviews can be conducted within a specified period of time, and a large volume of data can be collected within a short period of time.

These are other advantages of interviews:

- It is possible to obtain a detailed response from different categories of a sample population.
- More complex information can be collected.
- They are more personal than questionnaires and often produce better response rates, especially for more complex issues.
- The researcher may have more control over the question sequence and timing.
- Some questions can be adjusted in response to answers given to other questions.
- The researcher can explain some questions to the respondent in case of confusion, and thus ensure a better response.

However, interviews are often resource-intensive and at times are considered obtrusive, especially when personal questions and/or sensitive data are concerned. It can often take a considerable amount of time and skill to transcribe interviews and code the findings in a way that is suitable for analysis and interpretation. There are other factors to bear in mind:

- Information obtained through oral discussion may be difficult to analyse.
- Data may be qualitative rather than quantitative.
- There may be some inconsistency in the statements because some respondents may lose track of specifics over a long period of conversation.
- The respondent may be influenced or intimidated by the researcher.

When a number of interviewers are involved in a user study, it is important to ensure they all understand how the questions are to be put. Prompting should be used to ensure that respondents have considered all the possibilities when replying to questions.

Observation

Observation is a data collection instrument used for collecting qualitative data in user studies research that involves observing and recording events or situations. There are two forms of observation: participant and non-participant. In participant observation the researcher acts as a client or user to see what happens. In the non-participative mode, the researcher simply observes other people working and keeps a record. The observation method needs careful planning and often involves a lengthy process of securing permission for conducting the study, especially if it involves observation of real-life information systems, services or products. In observation methods there is no opportunity to steer the data collection process.

There are a number of advantages of this method:

- It is straightforward.
- It requires little training (though familiarization with the organization, institution or activity being observed is helpful).
- It provides direct experience.
- It provides useful insights to the existing system.
- It avoids bias that may occur in other methods of research.
- It does not make demands on the user's time.

However, there are certain obvious disadvantages to observation too:

- It may be obtrusive and those being observed may deviate from their normal behaviour if they know they are being observed.
- It may be time-consuming and the observer may have to wait for some time to see something happen, which could result in wasted time for the researcher.
- Some activities may involve several small steps and many activities are involved; sometimes it may be difficult to record events with every specific detail, particularly at busy periods.
- Record keeping may be inconsistent between different researchers.
- Transcription can take a lot of time.
- Researchers may not have detailed knowledge of the user or participant

contexts, such as specific activities for information requirements and use. As a result some of the events that take place during an observation may not be familiar to respondents, and therefore they may not understand what is happening.

- If more than one observer is involved, the results may be skewed depending on their interpretation.
- The constant attention and involvement of the researcher is needed.

Moreover, it is necessary that the researcher has an understanding of what to expect, what is going to be recorded and for what purpose. Often observation alone does not produce enough interpretable data, and therefore concurrent verbal accounts, or 'think aloud' protocols, may produce better results.

The think aloud method consists of asking people to think aloud while solving a problem and analysing the resulting verbal protocols (van Someren, Barnard and Sandberg, 1994). Think aloud protocols are now used commonly in usability studies where users are asked to say whatever they are looking at, thinking, doing and feeling as they perform their assigned task, and the researcher, observer in this case, takes note of, or records, whatever users say. Sometimes a talk aloud rather than a think aloud protocol is used where the participants are asked to discuss their actions without giving any explanations. Both think aloud and talk aloud protocols enrich the observation method by providing valuable information about users' actions and possible explanations of specific actions as they complete a task.

Focus groups

Originally called 'focused interviews', focus groups are structured group interviews that 'quickly and inexpensively reveal a target audience's desires, experiences and priorities' (Kuniavsky, 2003, 201). Focus groups are like a group discussions with 6–12 people in a group led by the researcher or facilitators. They are used to gather information about an event, product or service from the participants in their own words. They provide the researcher with 'a unique opportunity to see reality from the perspective of the user quickly, cheaply and (with careful preparation) easily' (Kuniavsky, 2003, 202). A variety of tools and techniques are used to capture data from focus groups. Sometimes sessions are recorded and/or notes are taken by the researcher or facilitator.

Focus groups as methods of user research have a number of advantages (Gorman and Clayton, 2005):

- *Speed*: It is possible to gather relevant information quickly from a number of people in the course of group discussions or one-to-one or one-to-many conversations.
- *Transparency*: Participants are told about the research objectives and they can see how the discussions are progressing, which encourages participation and engagement.
- *Interaction*: Participants interact with other participants and sometimes with the facilitator, which leads to better discussions and fruitful outcomes.
- *Flexibility*: Various issues, problems and possible suggestions are made, challenged and modified in the course of conversations, which provides more flexibility in research.
- *Open-endedness*: Open ended discussions may lead to unanticipated discovery of facts, leading to useful and valuable knowledge about a phenomenon.
- *Ability to note non-verbal communications*: The researcher or facilitator can note not only what is discussed but also non-verbal communications such as body language and gestures, which add more value to the points and information gathered.

Focus groups are very useful at the early stages of product or service development in order to evaluate preliminary concepts with potential users. They are also useful for proof of concept studies where a completely novel idea is discussed and/or tested among a group of potential users, or even to identify and confirm the characteristics of target users (Rubin and Chisnell, 2008). However, Kuniavsky (2003) warned that focus groups are not useful in situations where it is important to prove a point or to justify a position among a set of contesting ideas or contentious issues, and often focus groups are used in combination with other methods of data collection. Gorman and Clayton (2005) mentioned the following disadvantages of focus groups:

- *Getting people together*: It is always difficult to get a group of participants all at the same time and place at the participants' convenience.
- *Dominating personalities*: It is the role of the facilitator to make sure that everyone in a focus group gets a chance to speak out and offer their opinions or suggestions, but this may not always happen because some participants may have dominating personalities and steal the show.

- *Wanting to be agreeable*: A general tendency to come to an agreement is common in normal meetings, but focus groups do not always aim to generate agreeable solutions; often contesting views and conflicting opinions provide researchers with more insight into issues and problems.
- *Finding a typical group*: Forming a group of participants that is representative of the entire population is not always easy, and yet getting a mixed group of participants is essential. However, sometimes it is difficult to manage a mixed group of people, especially if they are from the same organization, because some junior or younger members may feel intimated by those who are senior or older.

It should be noted that as a focus group is a qualitative research method, it produces results that cannot be statistically presented or measured in order to produce generalizable data for a larger population. However, they can be used to create generalized models based on observations by a researcher. Kuniavsky (2003) identified different types of focus group, those that:

- *Are exploratory*: These are designed to gather general requirements and attitudes of users on a given topic, towards a specific product or service. The findings are helpful for designers at the early stage of their design of information products or services.
- *Prioritize features*: These are conducted to gather information about a specific information product or service. They focus on which features are more or less attractive to users and why.
- *Analyse competition*: These are conducted to gather information on comparable information products and services. They are designed to gather information – which features users like and which they don't – and thus gather competitive market intelligence.
- *Explain trends*: These aim to understand users' motivations and expectations from an information product and service. They are generally held either as part of a redesign process or in response to specific issues related to an information product or service.

Diaries

In a diary study, respondents are asked to keep a diary as they use an information service or product. In some cases they keep simple notes of action, in others they are encouraged to keep reflective logs that can be used to trace how often they used the product or service, what mistakes they made, what they learnt, and so on. Usually diary entries are kept for a specific period of time – one week, two weeks and so on. On completion of the study period, the diaries are coded and analysed to determine usage patterns.

Kuniavsky (2003) described how diaries can be structured or unstructured:

- Unstructured diary studies are often open ended and participant-driven, where the participants relate their everyday experiences, tracking their learning and the problems they encounter as and when they encounter them.
- Structured diary studies are somewhat controlled by the researcher where, under the remote guidance of the researchers or a moderator, users perform specific tasks and use or examine specific aspects of the information product or service, reporting their experiences in a diary format predetermined by the researcher.

Diaries can reveal very useful data because they record the actions and viewpoints of individual participants; even with minimal analysis they can provide a set of rich data, which would be difficult to obtain otherwise. They are unobtrusive, and participants can record actions and reactions in their own way as they perform their daily activities. Diary studies are one of few geographically distributed qualitative research methods: a variety of users at different locations may fill their diaries at the same or different times. However, it can be difficult to get a group of users who are willing voluntarily to participate in this method of research because people are too busy to keep notes of their activities, decisions and so on while carrying out their daily work. Often the notes contain context-specific actions and jargon, for example in specific fields like medicine and healthcare, research labs and so on, which may be difficult to code and analyse by researchers who do not have a good background in the domain and context.

Transaction log analysis

Most information products and services are now available online, and users can keep records of their usage on the web through transaction logs, which provide a set of rich data telling us what users have used (or not), for how long, and how their activities and movements have taken place while they were online (using the service or product). Transaction logs supply contextual and real-life data on the usage of an information product or service. Web servers keep records of every activity users have made, and access logs can yield very useful information:

- *where a request came from*: information about the user, which can be traced through the internet protocol (IP) address, location and so on
- *what the request was*: data on what type of information was requested, for example a specific web page or file from a given site, a new site and so on; this can tell us which part of an information product or service has been accessed, when the user moved from one section of the product or service to another, and when the user moved to a new site
- *when it was requested*: the date and time the request was made, which can be used to determine when and for how long a specific page (an aspect of a service or product) has been used
- *what browser was making the request*
- *what operating system the browser was running*
- *the server status code*: telling us whether the server was able to deliver the web page or file
- *the referrer*: indicating the page and site that a user viewed immediately before making the current request.

There are several advantages of log analysis as a method of studying user behaviour in the context of an information product or service. First, they provide a huge volume of data and often for a large user population over a period of time. Second, this is an unobtrusive method of data collection and the necessary data can be gathered easily. What makes web log analysis unique is 'its capability to yield data of truly enormous reach and detail, for logs record each use of everyone who happens to engage with the system' (Nicholas and Herman, 2009, 153). Compared with other methods of data collection, log analysis paints a true picture of what users have done in relation to a specific information product or service rather than what they wished or would have done in a specific situation or condition. Thus logs provide real-life data, which can be analysed to get a true picture of the usage patterns of an information product or service. Data can be collected routinely and automatically without the intervention of humans, and thus longitudinal studies can be conducted to see changes in the usage patterns, if any, over a period of time.

However, log analysis as a method has its pitfalls:

- This method enables researchers to reach only actual users, and not potential or non-users.
- It can only tell us what users have done at a given point in time, but not why they have done so, or what was going through their minds in the course of those actions.
- Analysis of data from transaction logs can be time-consuming and painstaking.

Often, it may not be possible to track a particular user because at best one can identify the IP address of a computer and so unless it is planned properly and a way of tracking a specific person or group of users behind an IP address is predetermined, it is not possible to draw conclusions on specific user behaviour. This often becomes difficult because of dynamic IP addresses where a specific computer is given an IP address automatically as it is available at the time of day. Thus the same user logging in at different times of the day may have a different IP address every time, and since through transaction logs we can only see an IP address and assume that it is linked to a specific computer, and thus to a specific user using that computer, for dynamic IP addresses it is difficult to trace the user through the IP address because every time it changes.

It can be difficult to differentiate between a human user and a computer user such as a search engine robot, as often the transactions are logged exactly the same way as they would be for a human user. In an attempt to overcome these drawbacks Nicholas and his associates at the CIBER research group (see for example, Nicholas, Huntington and Watkinson, 2005; Nicholas, Huntington and Jamali, 2008) have developed a 'deep log analysis' technique that uses triangulation of methods to generate useful data about the true usage patterns of a web-based information product or service.

Summary

Introduced for the first time in 1948, user studies has remained a major area of research over the past six decades, and information need has remained a major area of study within the field of user studies; many researchers have proposed models to identify and analyse user information needs in different contexts. A variety of qualitative and quantitative approaches and methods of data collection techniques have been employed by researchers for conducting user studies and studying information needs and user information behaviour. Despite these myriad research studies, many questions and issues remain unexplored, and the challenges have become more severe following the emergence and proliferation of new technologies and services including the web, social networks and a myriad of new information products and services that have appeared on the web over the past few years. Some of the issues and challenges (with special reference to usability studies) of information products and services are discussed in the subsequent chapters of this book.

References

Bawden, D. (2008) Users, User Studies and Human Information Behaviour: a three-decade perspective on Tom Wilson's 'On user studies and information needs', *Journal of Documentation*, special issue, 187–95.

Belkin, N. J. (1980) Anomalous States of Knowledge as a Basis for Information Retrieval, *Canadian Journal of Information Science*, 5, 133–43.

Gorman, G. E. and Clayton, P. (eds) (2005) *Qualitative Research for the Information Professional: a practical handbook*, 2nd edn, Facet Publishing.

Gunter, B., Rowlands, I. and Nicholas, D. (2009) *Is There a Google Generation?: information search behaviour developments and the future learner*, Chandos Publishing.

Hepworth, M. (2007) Knowledge of Information Behaviour and its Relevance to the Design of People-Centred Information Products and Services, *Journal of Documentation*, **63** (1), 33–56.

Hjørland, B. (2000) User Studies, www.iva.dk/bh/core%20concepts%20in%20lis/articles%20a-z/user_studies.htm.

Ingwersen, P. (1996) Cognitive Perspectives of Information Retrieval Interaction: elements of a cognitive IP theory, *Journal of Documentation*, **52** (1), 3–50.

Kuhlthau, C. (2004) *Seeking Meaning: a process approach to library and information services*, 2nd edn, Libraries Unlimited.

Kuniavsky, M. (2003) *Observing the User Experience: a practitioner's guide to user research*, Morgan Kaufmann.

Maslow, A. (1954) *Motivation and Personality*, Harper.

Nicholas, D. and Herman, E. (2009) *Assessing Information Needs in the Age of the Digital Consumer*, 3rd edn, Routledge.

Nicholas, D., Huntington, P. and Jamali, H. R. (2008) User Diversity: as demonstrated by deep log analysis, *The Electronic Library*, **26** (1), 21–38.

Nicholas, D., Huntington, P. and Watkinson, A. (2005) Scholarly Journal Usage: the results of deep log analysis, *Journal of Documentation*, **61** (2), 248–80.

Niedźwiedzka, B. (2003) A Proposed General Model of Information Behaviour, *Information Research*, **9** (1), paper 164.

Rowlands, I., Nicholas, D., Williams, P., Huntington, P. and Fieldhouse, M. (2008) The Google Generation: the information behaviour of the researcher of the future, *Aslib Proceedings: New Information Perspectives*, **60** (4), 209–310.

Rubin, J. and Chisnell, D. (2008) *Handbook of Usability Testing: how to plan, design and conduct effective tests*, 2nd edn, Wiley Publishing.

Saracevic, T. (1997) The Stratified Model of Information Retrieval Interaction: extension and applications, *Proceedings of the American Society for Information Science*, **34**, 313–27.

Taylor, R. (1991) Information Use Environments, *Progress in Communication Science*, **10**, 217–51.

van Someren, M. W., Barnard, Y. F. and Sandberg, J. A. C. (1994) The Think Aloud Method: a practical guide to modelling cognitive processes, Academic Press.

Wilson, T. D. (1981) On User Studies and Information Needs, *Journal of Documentation*, **37** (1), 3–15.

Wilson, T. D. (1999) Models in Information Behaviour Research, *Journal of Documentation*, **55** (3), 249–70.

Wilson, T. D. (2000) Recent Trends in User Studies: action research and qualitative methods, *Information Research*, **5** (3).

Wilson, T. D. (2008) On User Studies and Information Needs, *Journal of Documentation*, special issue, 174–86.

Xie, I. (2008) *Interactive Information Retrieval in Digital Environments*, IGI Publishing.

3

Human information behaviour studies and models

Introduction

Over 10,000 articles have been published on different aspects of human information behaviour (HIB) research and there has been a steady growth since 2000: '30 items per year during the early 1970s, 40 during the early 1980s, 50 by the late 1980s, 100 by 1990, and 120 items per year by 2005' (Case, 2007, 242). Keeping track of such a rapidly growing literature is a challenging task. Fortunately, a representative range of literature has been reviewed in several publications including:

- '60 Years of the Best in Information Research on User Studies and Information Needs' by Wilson (2006b)
- 'Users, User Studies and Human Information Behaviour: a three decade perspective on Tom Wilson's "On user studies and information needs"' by Bawden (2006)
- A chapter in *Annual Review of Information Science and Technology*, 'Information Behavior' by Case (2006)

In addition, a number of sources have emerged which deal exclusively or predominantly with information seeking, for example:

- Information Seeking in Context (ISIC) conference series since 1996
- special issues of several journals including *Informing Science* (**3** (2), 2000), *Journal of the American Society for Information Science and Technology* (**55** (8), 2004), *Journal of Documentation* (**62** (6), 2006, and **63** (1), 2007), *Information Processing & Management* ('Designing for Uncertainty', 2008) and *Library & Information Science Research* (**23** (4), 2001)

- the electronic journal *Information Research* (http://informationr.net/ir/), edited and published by T. D. Wilson
- a number of recent books including: *Looking for Information* (Case, 2007), *New Directions in Human Information Behaviour* (Spink and Cole, 2005), *The Turn* (Ingwersen and Jarvelin, 2005) and *Theories of Information Behaviour* (Fisher, Erdelez and McKechnie, 2006).

The chapter begins with the definition of HIB, and information seeking and retrieval. It sets the overall background of HIB study in general, then discusses the concept of information seeking and retrieval, which is a subset of HIB research, and an important aspect of usability of information products and services. Several models in the literature aim to provide a theoretical underpinning of HIB and the information seeking and retrieval process, focusing particularly on human aspects. Therefore, some widely used information seeking behaviour models and some new models derived from recent research work are discussed in this chapter. The new information seeking models will offer some insights of new directions of information behaviour research. Overall, the discussions on the selected models presented in this chapter indicate what researchers have said about the cognitive aspects of information seeking and retrieval. This will help us understand the impact of HIB research and the resulting models on information seeking in the modern electronic information environment, which has a significant bearing on usability research.

Human information behaviour

Taylor (1991, 221) defined information behaviour as 'the sum of activities through which information becomes useful'. Wilson (2000, 49) defined information behaviour in a wider sense, through which he linked the human condition and information together, as 'the totality of human behaviour in relation to sources and channels of information, including both active and passive information seeking, and information use'. Pettigrew, Fidel and Bruce (2001, 44) commented that information behaviour is 'how people need, seek, give and use information in different contexts'. Davenport (1997, 83) provided a more comprehensive definition of HIB, especially from the perspectives of information management, by saying that HIB is 'how individuals approach and handle information. This includes searching for it, using it, modifying it, sharing it, hoarding it, even ignoring it. Consequently, when we manage information behaviour, we're attempting to improve the overall effectiveness of an organization's information environment through concerted action.'

It is important to note that information behaviour 'encompasses information seeking and the totality of other unintentional or passive behaviours (such as glimpsing or encountering information) as well as purposive behaviours that do not involve seeking such as actively avoiding information' (Case, 2007, 5). Nevertheless, we are constantly adapting ourselves for information acquisition in the fast changing digital environment.

Information seeking and retrieval

People engage in information seeking behaviour because their current state of knowledge is inadequate to resolve some problem, or achieve some goal (Belkin, 2000). Marchionini (1995, 5) defined information seeking as 'a process in which humans purposefully engage in order to change their state of knowledge', adding (1995, 6) that 'information seeking is a fundamental human process closely related to learning and problem solving', and it is a 'high level cognitive process'. Many other researchers express similar views. For example, Case (2007, 333) observed that information seeking is a 'behaviour that occurs when an individual senses a problematic situation or information gap, in which his or her internal knowledge and beliefs, and model of the environment, fail to suggest a path towards satisfaction of his or her goals'. Information seeking research and theory is increasingly focusing on the role of information behaviour and its impact on cognitive behaviour (Nahl, 2004).

Some researchers prefer the term information seeking and retrieval (often referred to in the literature as IS&R) to information seeking. Ingwersen and Jarvelin (2005, 31) stated:

> With reference to the cognitive viewpoint information is one of the most central
> phenomena of interest to information seeking and retrieval and information
> science in general. Understanding this phenomenon is an imperative for
> enhancing our conception of other central phenomena, such as, information need
> formation and development, relevance, or knowledge representation, acquisition
> and use.

Vakkari and Jarvelin (2005, 114) identified the goals of information seeking and retrieval research as: '(a) theoretically understanding information seeking and retrieval in the form of models and theories, (b) empirically describing and explaining IS&R in various contexts, and (c) providing support in the design of information systems and information management in various contexts'.

Models in human information behaviour and information seeking and retrieval

Models focus on more specific problems than do theories (Case, 2007). Wilson (1999a, 250) suggested:

> A model may be described as a framework for thinking about a problem and may evolve into a statement of the relationships among theoretical propositions. Most models in the general field of information behaviour are of the former variety: they are statements, often in the form of diagrams, that attempt to describe an information-seeking activity, the causes and consequences of the activity, or the relationships among stages in information-seeking behaviour.

Many models have been proposed to strengthen research in HIB. Existing models were developed with a specific need, but models represent in general how people seek, search, organize, use information and encounter problems, if any, through diagrams and/or flowcharts. In the next sections, some widely used HIB and ISR models – those of Belkin (1980), Belkin et al. (1995), Saracevic (1997), Spink (1997), Wilson (1999a), Kuhlthau (1993), Ellis (1989) and Ingwersen (1996) – and some new models in the digital environment – proposed by Chowdhury (2008), Choo, Detlor and Turnbull (1999), Niedźwiedzka (2003), Pharo (2004) and Ford (2004) – are discussed.

Belkin's anomalous state of knowledge model

The essence of Belkin's (1980) anomalous state of knowledge (ASK) model is that an information need arises from a recognized anomaly in the user's state of knowledge concerning some topic or situation, and that, in general, the user is unable to specify precisely what is needed to resolve that anomaly. Anomaly in Belkin's (1980) model is defined as a state of inadequacy, which could result from lack of knowledge or one of many other problems, such as uncertainty as to which of several potentially relevant concepts holds in a given situation. Therefore, it is more important to attempt to describe that anomalous state of knowledge than to ask the user to specify the need as a request to the system.

The underlying concept in Belkin's (1980) model is that there exists a universe of texts that have been generated by a large number of human beings. The actual communication begins when the recipient engages with one or more texts and thereby completes the communication system; the process terminates when some goal has been achieved. There are two levels of communications in Belkin's model – at the linguistic level generators produce texts that users read; and at the cognitive level the texts are understood as representing the conceptual states of knowledge of their generators. Recipients' understanding is modified by their purposes, values, intentions, beliefs and state of knowledge (Figure 3.1). The model focuses fundamentally on an individual's cognitive approach (Figure 3.1) and people might experience different information needs in the same situations depending on their cognitive viewpoint.

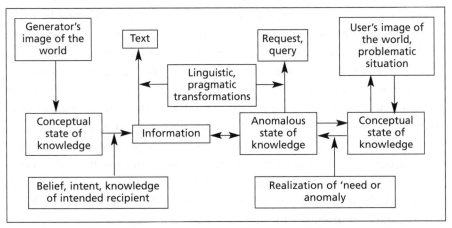

Figure 3.1 *The communication system of interest to information science (Belkin, 1980, 135)*

Belkin et al.'s episode model

Belkin et al.'s (1995) proposed episode model suggests that user interaction with an information retrieval system takes place as a sequence of different interactions in an episode of information seeking. The focus of this model is on the design of information retrieval systems in that it focuses on the actions carried out in an information search, method of interaction (scanning–searching) or goal of interaction (learning–selecting); mode of retrieval (recognition–specification); and resource considered (information–meta-information). According to this model, information seeking strategies arise from users' problem situation, more specifically from users' state of knowledge and information seeking goal. Thus the variety of behaviour people engage in while searching for information in some knowledge resource can be viewed as information seeking strategies calling for interactions between the user and the components of the information retrieval system (Belkin et al., 1995).

Saracevic's model

Saracevic's stratified interaction model is described in Chapter 2 (Figure 2.4). It was developed within an overall framework of an 'acquisition-cognition-application' model of information use. It has three level or strata: cognitive, affective and situational (Saracevic, 1997).

On the cognitive level, the user interacts with the output of the system, through one or more system interactions, in ways that enable the user to assess the utility of the search output in relation to the search problem. The user interprets and judges the search output and assimilates them cognitively.

The user interacts with their intentions, such as beliefs, motivation, feelings (for example frustration), urgency and so on, at the affective level. A user interacts with a system through an interface by issuing commands or queries that in some way represent a problem statement. Investigation of analysing users' intentions, beliefs and motivations go on at this level.

At the situational level, the user interacts with the given problem in hand, which arises from the information need. Therefore the results of the search may be useful to resolve the problem partially or completely. The user judges the output obtained based on the problem in hand, changes in the problem, categorization of problems for interactive decisions, and so on.

Saracevic (1997) emphasized:

The situation that was the reason for interaction to start with, produced a problem that sometimes may be well sometimes ill defined, and the related question, if not on paper then in [a] user's mind, may also be defined in various well-ill degrees. In addition, a user also brings a given knowledge or cognitive state related to the situation, as well as an intentionality – these also may be well or ill defined. All this is used on the surface level to specify and modify queries, select files, search terms, search tactics, and other attributes to use in searching and decision-making, and on the deeper, cognitive level to interpret and otherwise cognitively process the texts, and make or change relevance inferences and other decisions.

Spink's feedback model

Spink (1997) proposed a model of the information search process, which identifies user judgements, search tactics or moves, interactive feedback loops, and cycles as constituting the search process of a person in interaction with an information retrieval system. According to this model each search strategy may consist of one or more cycles of search, and each cycle may consist of one or more occurrences of interactions such as user input, information retrieval system output, user interpretation and judgement, and further user input, if necessary. Furthermore, Spink (1997) suggests that a user input may also represent a move within the search strategy and it may be regarded as a search tactic to further the search.

Wilson's model

Wilson's model is widely considered to be one of the most comprehensive explanations of information seeking behaviour (see Chapter 2, Figure 2.3). It portrays the cycle of information activities from the rise of information need until the information is used. It identifies some intervening variables, which have a significant influence on information behaviour, and mechanisms which activate it. The rise of a particular need is influenced by the context, which can be the person or the role the person plays in work and life, or environment (social, political, economical, technological and so on).

Kuhlthau's model

Kuhlthau (1993) suggested an affective orientation to the information search process. She views information seeking as a process of construction in which users progress from uncertainty to understanding; in other words, uncertainty is reduced through this process. Kuhlthau's model (Figure 3.2 overleaf) is based on a longitudinal study of high school students.

Kuhlthau identified a six stage process:

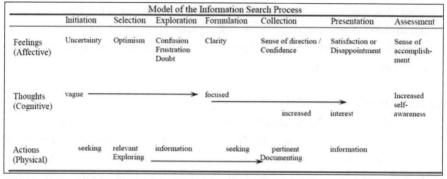

Figure 3.2   *Kuhlthau's model (Kuhlthau, 2004, 82)*

- *initiation*: when a person first becomes aware of a lack of knowledge or understanding, and feelings of uncertainty and apprehension trigger a need for information
- *selection*: when a general area, topic or problem is identified and initial uncertainty often gives way to a brief sense of optimism and a readiness to begin the search
- *exploration*: when inconsistent, incompatible information is encountered and uncertainty, confusion and doubt frequently increase
- *formulation*: when a focused perspective is formed and uncertainty diminishes as confidence begins to increase, resulting in a change in feelings with indications of increased confidence and a sense of clarity
- *collection*: when interaction between the user and the information system takes place, the main activity being to gather information related to the query, and feelings of confidence continue to increase as uncertainty subsides, with the identification of relevant information
- *presentation*: when the search is completed; there is a sense of satisfaction if the search has gone well or disappointment if it has not.

Kuhlthau (1993) also proposed that uncertainty is a principle for information seeking. Her model emphasizes the 'holistic' view of information transfer, which incorporates the experience of interacting thoughts, actions and feelings in the process of construction. Later Kuhlthau (2004, 92) emphasized that uncertainty initiates the process, and anxiety and an unsettling discomfort may be experienced in the early stages, but 'as knowledge states shift to more clearly focused thoughts, a parallel shift occurs in feelings of increased confidence'. A similar view has been expressed by Belkin in his ASK model (Figure 3.1).

The information seeking process presents information seeking as a process of construction influenced by George Kelly's personal construct theory (Kuhlthau, 2004). Kuhlthau's model is the first to investigate the affective behaviour (relating to feelings) of a person along with the cognitive (thought-related) and physical (action and strategy-related) aspects in the process of information seeking. However, Kuhlthau's model focuses on the information search process rather than on how users use and evaluate the retrieved information.

Ellis's model

Ellis's (1989) behavioural model has the following categories of information seeking and retrieval activities that may or may not occur in a sequence:

- *starting*: identifying relevant sources of interest
- *chaining*: following and connecting new leads found in an initial source
- *browsing*: scanning contents of identified sources for subject affinity
- *differentiating*: filtering and assessing sources for usefulness
- *monitoring*: keeping abreast of developments in a given subject area
- *extracting*: selectively identifying relevant material in an information source, or systematically working through a given source for material of interest
- *verifying*: checking the accuracy of information
- *ending*: 'tying up loose ends' through a final search.

Wilson (1999a) observed that Kuhlthau's model is more general than that of Ellis in drawing attention to the feelings associated with the various stages and activities and (1999a, 257) that 'it is fairly obvious that the models of both Ellis and Kuhlthau relate to the active search mode of information-seeking behaviour'.

Ingwersen's model

Ingwersen's model (1996) shows the relations among information and cognitive processes. The model incorporates the socio-organizational environment (context) of the current searcher with the information retrieval interaction. The context, in this model, includes the scientific or professional domain(s) with information preferences, strategies and work tasks that influence the existing perception of the searcher. The 1992 model had been expanded in 1996 by including the work task or cultural–emotional interest and corresponding situation as perceived by a searcher. He suggested that various cognitive transformations, starting from recognition of a new problem to the situation where information objects are searched and useful ones are identified in a retrieval system, take place within the cognitive space (Figure 3.3). Ingwersen's (1996) cognitive model integrates ideas relating to information behaviour with issues of information retrieval system design. The idea of polyrepresentation is an important strength of the model.

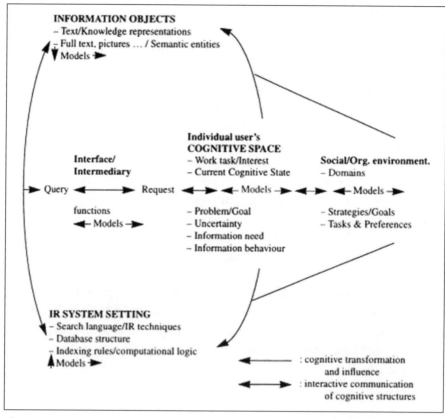

Figure 3.3   *Ingwersen's model (Ingwersen, 1996)*

Information seeking on the web

Seeking information and, in particular, tracing relevant information on the web is a complex task because the same information is diffused, appears in various forms, and is available through different channels. Information seeking on the web is a topic of increasing interest in many disciplines. Because of fast changing technologies and information overload, searching and evaluating appropriate information has become a key requirement for success in the digital era. While various organizations and individuals are trying to improve the accessibility of information on the web by developing sophisticated retrieval tools, users' interactions remain important, because retrieving an immense volume of information in response to a web search may influence users' cognitive behaviour. Some recent research work in information seeking behaviour, especially in the context of digital environment, is discussed below.

Some researchers suggest that while seeking information on the web users adopt different strategies because of their varying cognitive styles (see Dilevko and Gottlieb, 2004; Kari, 2006; Kari and Savolainen, 2007; Frias-Martinez, Chen and Liu, 2008; and Thatcher, 2008). Therefore, the information seeking and retrieval process is highly variable because it significantly differs from person to person. Several studies on information seeking in the context of teaching and/or learning have been reported in the recent past (see for example Talja, 2002; Pennanen and Vakkari, 2003; Ford, 2004; Hemminger et al., 2007; Olander, 2007; and Jansen, Booth and Smith, 2009).

Some researchers propose a contextual model of web searching from an individual's perspective (Kari and Savolainen, 2003); others report on end users' web information behaviour (Markey, 2007a, 2007b) and the dynamics of interactive information retrieval behaviour (Xu, 2007); while others focus on several web-based task categories and the differences in how participants interact with their web browsers across the range of information-seeking tasks (Kellar, Watters and Shepherd, 2007), multitasking information seeking and searching on the web (Spink, Ozmutlu and Ozmutlu, 2002), and the importance of context in information seeking and retrieval (Kelly, 2006a, 2006b).

Several researchers have focused on the web information seeking activities of different types of users – web information seeking behaviour of women in the IT profession (Choo and Marton, 2003); how users' cognitive (characteristic way of organizing and processing information) and affective (emotional) characteristics influence the navigational and search behaviours on the web among experienced web users (Kim and Allen, 2002; Kim, 2005); the effect of students' web search experiences for locating an appropriate website and retrieving relevant information (Lazonder, Biemans and Wopereis, 2000); the method for analysing searching behaviour (Pharo and

Jarvelin, 2004); and the problem of judging information quality and cognitive authority by observing people's information seeking behaviour on the web (Rieh, 2002). A number of individual criteria including specificity, topicality, familiarity and variety are used most frequently in relevance judgements (Savolainen and Kari, 2006). A new analysis and display tool is used to examine the influences of understanding the system and goals of end-user web searching (Slone, 2002); because of the proliferation of information and the variety of means of retrieval, it is vital to understand why some searchers are more successful than others (Tabatabai and Shore, 2005).

A number of studies have also been undertaken on information seeking in different domains other than information science, such as health (Doney, 2005; Ankem, 2006; Hughes, 2010), engineering (Kerins, Madden and Fulton, 2004), law (Kuhlthau and Tama, 2001; Makri, Blandford and Cox, 2008), journalism (Attfield and Dowell, 2003), sports (Joinson and Banyard, 2002), everyday life (Agosto and Hughes-Hassell, 2005) and specific problems (Savolainen, 2007, 2008).

Some new information seeking behaviour models

Spink and Jansen (2004, 28) observed that 'web search behaviour studies have proliferated in number and complexity, and are becoming more international and interdisciplinary in nature. The range of studies has diversified to include cognitive and behaviour studies using transaction log, experimental, single web site and longitudinal studies.' Emphasizing the importance of HIB studies in the context of the modern digital information era, Wilson (2006a, 683) commented,

> Electronic information resources, structured in various ways, are becoming the dominant environment within which information seeking takes place and, consequently, the current engagement with the relationship between seeker and the world wide web, digital libraries and other information structures is likely to continue.

Some of the new models proposed by Chowdhury (2008), Choo, Detlor and Turnbull (1999), Niedźwiedzka (2003), Pharo (2004) and Ford (2004) discussed in the next section provide a glimpse of the new directions of information seeking behaviour research, especially in the context of digital environment.

Chowdhury's new uncertainty model

Uncertainty in the field of information seeking research is normally associated with the experiences of the searcher. Kuhlthau (2004, 103) defined uncertainty as 'a cognitive state that commonly causes affective symptoms of anxiety and lack of confidence'. So, the question remains: what causes uncertainty in information seeking and retrieval in a digital environment and what are the implications of such uncertainty? Kuhlthau (2004) pointed out that uncertainty decreases when the searcher proceeds towards the completion of the search process. Wilson et al. (2000, 2002) agreed with Kuhlthau that uncertainty decreases, but also argued that at any of the four stages of Wilson's model (Wilson, 1999b) – problem recognition, problem definition, problem resolution and solution statement – uncertainty may arise and successive searches within the same stage, or any other stage, may be required to resolve the problem. Wilson (1999b) hypothesized that there is a successive resolution of more and more uncertainty while a search proceeds from one stage to another; where uncertainty fails to be resolved at any one stage, it may be resolved through the feedback loop to the previous stage. Kuhlthau (2004, 8) commented that 'an information search is a learning process in which the choices along the way are dependent on personal constructs rather than on one universal, predictable search for everyone'. This statement reinforces the fact that information seeking and retrieval is an individual process, and therefore it is difficult to prepare a universal search strategy. Furthermore, Yovits and Foulk (1985) found that information may increase a person's uncertainty level in a particular situation.

Researchers have expressed similar views in the context of web information seeking and retrieval. Ramirez et al. (2002) argued that the existing theory and research on computer-mediated communication provides a limited view of information seeking behaviour and uncertainty. Sias and Wyers (2001) explained that while information may reduce an employee's uncertainty about a specific issue, subsequent events may cause that employee to feel uncertain about another issue. Thus, uncertainty is a natural and pervasive aspect of any employee's working life, whether a newcomer or a veteran. Nahl (2006) stated that when people operate with ineffective cognitive behaviours, the affective load, such as cognitive ambiguity, uncertainty or information overload, is invariably high and attracts affective behaviours that are negative and counter productive to the searcher's goal. For example, a searcher is cognitively disoriented if no relevant results are produced after several attempts. Attfield et al. (2008) noted that web information seekers are frequently uncertain about the information they want and, in the context of news research and writing, as users proceed through cycles of information acquisition, assimilation and use, they create and maintain personal and informal collections of information.

It may be stated that the generally held view in HIB research is that uncertainty is a mental state of users reflecting a gap in knowledge, which triggers an information seeking and retrieval process, and the gap is filled as relevant information is found, and thus the uncertainty disappears as the search process concludes. As well as the gap in the mind of a user with reference to the knowledge about a given subject or topic, the various complexities associated with the information seeking and retrieval process in the digital environment can cause uncertainty among users (Chowdhury and Gibb, 2009). In other words, the complex activities and processes involved in information seeking and retrieval in the electronic environment may make the user unsure of the outcome of a search process, and thus may add to their uncertainty (Chowdhury, Gibb and Landoni, 2011). The findings of this research (Chowdhury, 2008) showed that uncertainty occurs for a number of information seeking activities and problems, and that such uncertainty may continue in the course of successive search sessions, until a new uncertainty model has been developed (Figure 3.4). The uncertainty model is unique because:

- It shows that in the digital environment uncertainty may be caused by a number of information seeking activities and problems.
- Such uncertainty may persist in the course of a series of search sessions, although there may be a shift in uncertainty.
- While there are negative implications of such uncertainty, there are some positive implications as well.

Figure 3.4 provides a conceptual representation of the new uncertainty model showing that uncertainty may occur in the course of several information seeking activities and problems. The model shows that a user's information need triggers an information seeking and retrieval process that involves a number of information seeking activities and problems that can be derived from the various stages of information seeking (Chowdhury, 2008). It proposes that as the searcher goes through an information seeking and retrieval process, various information seeking activities and problems may cause different degrees of uncertainty, and that such uncertainty may persist

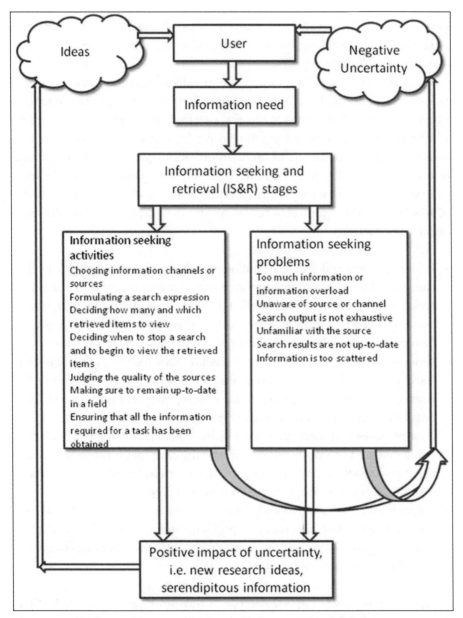

Figure 3.4   *The uncertainty model in information seeking and retrieval*

even after a series of information searches. Thus the basic tenet of the model is that some form of uncertainty is always present in information seeking and retrieval in the digital environment. Although the extent of such uncertainty caused by specific information seeking activities and problems varies depending on the nature and characteristics of users, and the degree of uncertainty may shift from one factor to another in course of a series of search sessions, it seldom disappears.

However, the model shows that while negative uncertainty causes anxiety, lack of confidence and frustration among users, there is a positive impact of uncertainty as well. Findings of this research indicate that the positive impact of uncertainty is felt by information users in a number of ways, such as making accidental discovery of useful information, getting a new direction in research through discovery of new or related information, becoming more prepared for successive information seeking and retrieval processes (Chowdhury, 2008), and so on. These are the implications of this new uncertainty model:

- It identifies a number of information seeking activities and problems that cause continued uncertainty among users in the course of information seeking and retrieval. This knowledge will be useful for designing new and improved information systems. As Ingwersen and Jarvelin (2005, 379) pointed out, 'the practical fruit for society that the information seeking and retrieval research provides are improved tools, systems and social practices for information access, acquisition and use. These are needed in accomplishing work tasks, solving everyday problems of life, or fulfilling cultural or other leisure interests.'
- It emphasizes that there are some positive impacts of uncertainty, and while new and/or improved designs should have measures to reduce the negative impacts of uncertainty, provisions should be made to help users reap the benefits of the positive impacts of uncertainty.
- It opens a new vista of research for identifying the different types of information seeking activities and problems that may cause uncertainty in information seeking and retrieval among different categories of users in different domains and contexts.

Many researchers, such as Meyyappan, Chowdhury and Foo (2001, 2004), Tenopir, Hitchcock and Pillow (2003), Chowdhury (2004), Ford (2004), Kerins, Madden and Fulton (2004), Tenopir et al. (2006) and Chowdhury and Chowdhury (2007), have emphasized the need for improved information services and the importance of better information skills training and task-based information access systems in the learning and digital work environment. The new uncertainty model will give providers of information systems and services a better idea of which factors may cause uncertainty in information seeking and retrieval, and consequently how such an uncertainty may be reduced or removed altogether to create a better learning environment. However, further research needs to be conducted to validate this uncertainty model.

Choo, Detlor and Turnbull's behavioural model

Choo, Detlor and Turnbull (1999) developed a behavioural model of information seeking on the web. People engage themselves in modes of information seeking to support their daily work activities when searching on the web, varying from undirected viewing to formal searching that retrieves focused information for action or decision making. Their two-dimensional model of information seeking behaviour of the web combined Aguilar's modes of scanning and Ellis's seeking behaviours. Table 3.1 shows four modes of information seeking on the web: undirected viewing, conditioned viewing, informal search and formal search. Each mode of information seeking on the web is differentiated by the nature of information needs, seeking tactics and the purpose of information use (Figure 3.1). The table depicts how users relate their motivations (the strategies and reasons for viewing and searching) and moves (the tactics used to find and use information).

Table 3.1 *Behavioural model of information seeking on the web (Choo, Detlor and Turnbull, 1999)*

	Starting	Chaining	Browsing	Differentiating	Monitoring	Extracting
Undirected viewing	✓	✓				
Conditioned viewing			✓	✓	✓	
Informal search				✓	✓	✓
Formal search					✓	✓

Niedźwiedzka's new general human information behaviour model

The totality of information behaviour is submerged in a context that consists of Wilson's intervening variables – personal, role-related and environmental – in the new model. Niedźwiedzka (2003) said:

Such presentation of the relationship stresses the fact that these factors are always present and they influence the process at all its stages. The new model indicates also that the activating mechanisms can occur at each link of the chain of behaviour leading to acquiring and using information. The psychological theories explaining activating mechanisms were removed from the diagram not to negate or undermine their importance, but because they are part of the knowledge base behind the used concepts. In the new model, a phase of the need occurrence is separated from a phase of making a decision to seek information, which follows Wilson's comments and suggests that also at this stage the activating mechanisms can play a significant role. The phases of information seeking, selection/processing and information application also are separated, and the justification of this separation is the same: the importance of activating mechanisms in stopping or impelling the process. The cycle-like, dynamic character of the process, reflecting the necessary feedback loop, is preserved.

The model (Figure 3.5) shows two basic strategies of information seeking:

- A user seeks information personally.
- A user uses the help or services of other people.

Figure 3.5 indicates that a user can choose one, the other, or both strategies.

Pharo's search situation and transition model

The model focuses on the domain of the search situation and transition method schema to illustrate the conceptual model behind the tool, which is (Pharo, 2004):

> A methodical tool for analysing information behaviour which takes into account factors traditionally dealt with from an information retrieval (for example actions performed in the search process) or information seeking (for example work task) perspective. In addition, the article includes extracts from an empirical study which shows that it is possible to use the method schema to identify effects of work tasks on real search processes.

Pharo emphasized that

> each Situation and Transition signifies a way of treating information searching as

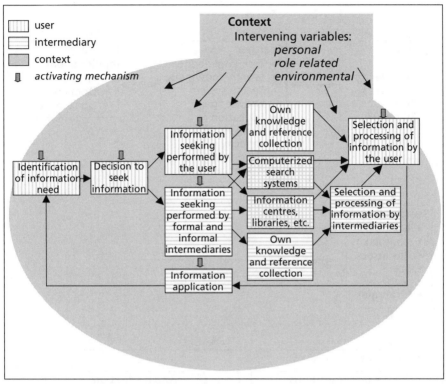

Figure 3.5   *A new general model of information behaviour (Niedźwiedzka, 2003)*

a process where a period of meta-data interaction (the transition) can be followed by a period of interaction with real data (the situation). The search process switches between interaction in these two data layers and is at the same time influenced by external factors, such as the work task, the searcher, his/her surroundings, and the search tasks generated by the work task.

Figure 3.6 overleaf shows the model's five main categories; the arrows indicate potential interplay between categories during the search process. Figure 3.6 also shows the integrating characteristics of the searcher, his or her surroundings, the work task, the search task, and the interaction process between searcher and search system.

Ford's model of learning-related information behaviour

Ford's (2004) model, presented in Figure 3.7 on page 75, emphasizes the

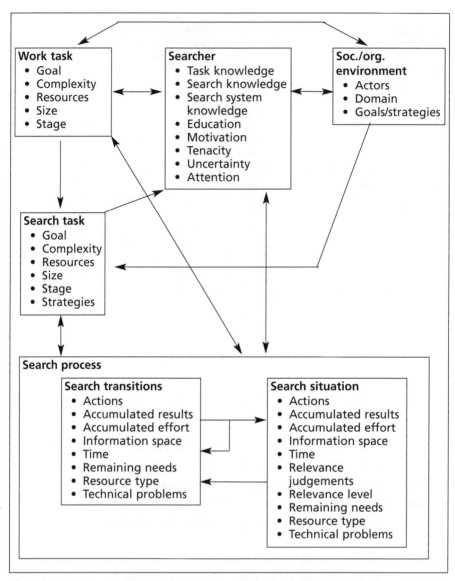

Figure 3.6 *The search situation and transition model (Pharo, 2004)*

complexity of information behaviour in the learning environment. It highlights the need for research into information behaviour to avoid an unrealistically narrow focus, and to take into account many interacting factors in the learning environment.

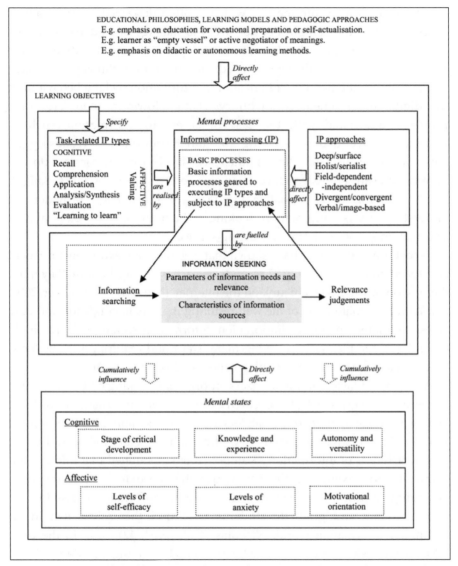

Figure 3.7 *A model of learning-related information behaviour (Ford, 2004)*

Summary

Human information behaviour is an area of multidisciplinary research, and researchers are always trying to find new ways of explaining information search behaviour of users especially in the emerging new digital environment. With the development of a wide variety of technologies, there is a constant flow of information, which is often described as irrelevant or excessive, or as too complicated for users to manage or understand (Case, 2007). We may all agree about certain advantages of the availability of a wide range of information through the advancement of technologies. Recent research shows there is a paradigm shift in information seeking behaviour in the digital environment (Chowdhury, 2008). However, there are some problems associated with the ease of access to information, such as information overload – receiving too much information (Klaussegger, Sinkovics and Zou, 2007). Other studies have shown that the constant flow of information can seriously reduce a person's ability to focus on tasks (Knight, 2005). Therefore it is a challenging task for information providers to understand users' information seeking behaviour and develop a new information service or improve existing services.

Recent usability studies have shown that web users are extremely impatient and spend an average of only 27 seconds on each web page because they think there is too much 'irrelevant junk on the internet' (Nielsen and Loranger, 2006, 22). With the proliferation of the web resulting in users having wide and easy access to a large amount of information, information seeking is increasingly becoming a complex task involving many steps and requiring various tools, task domains, systems and searching expertise (Komlodi, 2004).

A number of factors influence users' information seeking on the web, such as cognitive styles, search skills, search experience and information overload. Heimlich (2003) identified 13 barriers to the access and use of electronic sources; 'information overload' had the highest score followed by the 'trustworthiness of information'. Katopol (2006) mentioned that information overload and anxiety are the key issues that need to be considered in designing information systems to facilitate information seeking of undergraduate and graduate students who find themselves lost in an unfamiliar information world. Nicholas et al. (2004, 42) said: 'In the past, information seeking was seen to be the first step to creating knowledge. Now, it is no longer just a first step, it is a continuous process. Today, we probably ask the same question continuously, but of course against a constantly changing and evolving source list.'

Researchers across various disciplines have found that the performance (quality of decisions or reasoning in general) of individuals correlates positively with the amount of information they receive – to a certain extent (Eppler and Mengis, 2003). Therefore, users want not only to have easy access to information but also to be able to obtain it effortlessly (Melgoza, Mennel and Gyeszly, 2002). Fortunately information science researchers around the world, especially in the field of HIB, are building integrated frameworks that model different aspects of information seeking, retrieval and use. These new models, coupled with the existing knowledge of HIB and information seeking and retrieval, provide valuable information for researchers engaged in studying usability of information products and services.

References

Agosto, D. E. and Hughes-Hassell, S. (2005) People, Places, and Questions: an investigation of the everyday life information-seeking behaviors of urban young adults, *Library & Information Science Research*, **27** (2), 141–63.

Ankem, K. (2006) Use of Information Sources by Cancer Patients: results of a systematic review of the research literature, *Information Research*, **11** (3).

Attfield, S. and Dowell, J. (2003) Information Seeking and Use by Newspaper Journalists, *Journal of Documentation*, **59** (2), 187–204.

Attfield, S., Blandford, A., Dowell, J. and Cairns, P. (2008) Uncertainty-Tolerant Design: evaluating task performance and drag-and-link information gathering for a news-writing task, *International Journal on Human-Computer Studies*, **66**, 410–424.

Bawden, D. (2006) Users, User Studies and Human Information Behaviour: a three decade perspective on Tom Wilson's 'On user studies and information needs', *Journal of Documentation*, **62** (6), 671–79.

Belkin, N. J. (1980) Anomalous States of Knowledge as a Basis for Information Retrieval, *Canadian Journal of Information Science*, **5**, 133–43.

Belkin, N. J. (2000) Helping People Find What They Don't Know, *Communications of the ACM*, **43** (8), 58–61.

Belkin, N. J., Cool, C., Stein, A. and Thiel, U. (1995) Cases, Scripts and Information Seeking Strategies: on the design of interactive information retrieval systems, *Expert Systems with Applications*, **9** (3), 379–95.

Case, D. O. (2006) Information Behavior. In Cronin, B. (ed.), *Annual Review of Information Science and Technology*, Information Today, 293–328, 340.

Case, D. O. (2007) *Looking for Information: a survey of research on information seeking, needs and behaviour*, 2nd edn, Academic Press.

Choo, C. W. and Marton, C. (2003) Information Seeking on the Web by Women in IT Professions, *Internet Research: Electronic Networking Applications and Policy*, **13** (4), 267–80.

Choo, C. W., Detlor, B. and Turnbull, D. (1999) Information Seeking on the Web – an integrated model of browsing and searching. In *Proceedings of the 62nd Annual*

Meeting of the American Society of Information Science, Washington, D.C., Information Today.

Chowdhury, G. and Chowdhury, S. (2007) E-learning Support for LIS Education in UK, *7th Annual Conference of the Subject Centre for Information and Computer Sciences,* Higher Education Academy, 75–9.

Chowdhury, G. G. (2004) Access and Usability Issues of Scholarly Electronic Publications. In Gorman, G. E. and Rowland, F. (eds), *Scholarly Publishing in an Electronic Era: International Yearbook of Library and Information Management,* 2004–2005, Facet Publishing, 77–98.

Chowdhury, S. (2008) *Uncertainty in Information Seeking and Retrieval in the Context of Higher Education,* PhD thesis, University of Strathclyde, UK.

Chowdhury, S. and Gibb, F. (2009) Relationship Among Activities and Problems Causing Uncertainty in Information Seeking and Retrieval, *Journal of Documentation,* **65** (3), 470–99.

Chowdhury, S., Gibb, F. and Landoni, M. (2011) Uncertainty in Information Seeking and Retrieval: a study in an academic environment, *Information Processing and Management,* **47**, 157–75.

Davenport, T. (1997) *Information Ecology,* Oxford University Press.

Dilevko, J. and Gottlieb, L. (2004) Working at Tribal College and University Libraries: a portrait, *Library & Information Science Research,* **26** (1), 44–72.

Doney, L. (2005) Use of Libraries and Electronic Information Resources by Primary Care Staff: outcomes from a survey, *Health Information and Libraries Journal,* **22** (3), 182–88.

Ellis, D. (1989) A Behavioural Approach to Information Retrieval System Design, *Journal of Documentation,* **45** (3), 171–12.

Eppler, M. J. and Mengis, J. (2003) A Framework for Information Overload Research in Organizations: insights from organization science, accounting, marketing, MIS, and related disciplines, www.bul.unisi.ch/cerca/bul/pubblicazioni/com/pdf/wpca0301.pdf.

Fisher, K. E., Erdelez, S. and McKechnie, L. E. F. (eds) (2006) *Theories of Information Behaviour,* Information Today.

Ford, N. (2004) Towards a Model of Learning for Educational Informatics, *Journal of Documentation,* **60** (2), 183–225.

Frias-Martinez, E., Chen, S. and Liu, X. (2008) Investigation of Behavior and Perception of Digital Library Users: a cognitive style perspective, *International Journal of Information Management,* **28** (5), 355.

Heimlich, J. E. (2003) Environmental Educators on the Web: results of a national study of users and nonusers, *Journal of Environmental Education,* **34** (3), 4–11.

Hemminger, B. M., Lu, D., Vaughan, K. T. L. and Adams, S. J. (2007) Information Seeking Behavior of Academic Scientists, *Journal of the American Society for Information Science and Technology*, **58** (14), 2205–25.

Hughes, B. (2010) Doctors' Online Information Needs, Cognitive Search Strategies, and Judgments of Information Quality and Cognitive Authority: how predictive judgments introduce bias into cognitive search models, *Journal of the American Society for Information Science and Technology*, **61** (3), 433–52.

Ingwersen, P. (1996) Cognitive Perspectives of Information Retrieval Interaction: elements of a cognitive IP theory, *Journal of Documentation*, **52** (1), 3–50.

Ingwersen, P. and Jarvelin, K. (2005) *The Turn: integration of information seeking and retrieval in context*, Springer.

Jansen, B. J., Booth, D. and Smith, B. (2009) Using the Taxonomy of Cognitive Learning to Model Online Searching, *Information Processing & Management*, **45** (6), 643–63.

Joinson, A. and Banyard, P. (2002) Psychological Aspects of Information Seeking on the Internet, *Aslib Proceedings*, **54** (2), 95–102.

Kari, J. (2006) Free-Form Searching via Web Sites: content and moving observed in the context of personal development, *Information Processing and Management*, **42** (3), 769–84.

Kari, J. and Savolainen, R. (2003) Towards a Contextual Model of Information seeking on the Web, *New Review of Information Behaviour Research*, **4**, 155–75.

Kari, J. and Savolainen, R. (2007) Relationships Between Information Seeking and Context: a qualitative study of internet searching and the goals of personal development, *Library & Information Science Research*, **29** (1), 47–69.

Katopol, P. (2006) Library anxiety. In Fisher, K. E., Erdelez, S. and McKechnie, L. E. F. (eds), *Theories of Information Behaviour*, Information Today, 235–38.

Kellar, M., Watters, C. and Shepherd, M. (2007) A Field Study Characterizing Web-based Information-seeking Tasks, *Journal of the American Society for Information Science and Technology*, **58** (7), 999–1018.

Kelly, D. (2006a) Measuring Online Information Seeking Context, Part 1: background and method, *Journal of the American Society for Information Science and Technology*, **57** (13), 1729–39.

Kelly, D. (2006b) Measuring Online Information Seeking Context, Part 2: findings and discussion, *Journal of the American Society for Information Science and Technology*, **57** (14), 1862–74.

Kerins, G., Madden, R. and Fulton, C. (2004) Information Seeking and Students Studying for Professional Careers: the cases of engineering and law students in Ireland, *Information Research*, **10** (1), paper 208.

Kim, K. S. (2005) Experienced Web Users' Search Behavior: effects of focus and emotion control, *Proceedings American Society for Information Science and Technology*, **42**.

Kim, K. S. and Allen, B. (2002) Cognitive and Task Influences on Web Searching Behaviour, *Journal of the American Society for Information Science*, **53** (2), 109–19.

Klausegger, C., Sinkovics, R. and Zou, H. (2007) Information Overload: a cross-national investigation of influence factors and effects, *Marketing Intelligence & Planning*, **25** (7), 691–18.

Knight, W. (2005) 'Info-mania' Dents IQ More Than Marijuana, *New Scientist*, 22 April.

Komlodi, A. (2004) Task Management Support in Information Seeking: a case for search histories, *Computers in Human Behaviour*, **20**, 163–84.

Kuhlthau, C. (1993) A Principle of Uncertainty for Information Seeking, *Journal of Documentation*, **49** (4), 339–55.

Kuhlthau, C. (2004) *Seeking Meaning: a process approach to library and information services*, 2nd edn, Libraries Unlimited.

Kuhlthau, C. C. and Tama, S. L. (2001) Information Search Process of Lawyers: a call for 'just for me' information services, *Journal of Documentation*, **57** (1), 25–43.

Lazonder, A. W., Biemans, H. J. A. and Wopereis, I. G. J. H. (2000) Differences Between Novice and Experienced Users in Searching Information on the World Wide Web, *Journal of the American Society for Information Science*, **51** (6), 576–81.

Makri, S., Blandford, A. and Cox, A. L. (2008) Investigating the Information-Seeking Behaviour of Academic Lawyers: from Ellis's model to design, *Information Processing & Management*, **44** (2), 613–34.

Marchionini, G. (1995) *Information Seeking in Electronic Environments*, Cambridge University Press.

Markey, K. (2007a) Twenty-Five Years of End-User Searching, Part 1: research findings, *Journal of the American Society for Information Science and Technology*, **58** (8), 1071–81.

Markey, K. (2007b) Twenty-Five Years of End-User Searching, Part 2: future research directions, *Journal of the American Society for Information Science and Technology*, **58** (8), 1123–30.

Melgoza, P., Mennel, P. A. and Gyeszly, S. D. (2002) Information Overload, *Collection Building*, **21** (1), 32–43.

Meyyappan, N., Chowdhury G. G. and Foo, S. (2001) Use of a Digital Work Environment (DWE) Prototype to Create a User-Centred University Digital Library, *Journal of Information Science*, **27** (4), 249–64.

Meyyappan, N., Chowdhury G. G. and Foo, S. (2004) Design and Evaluation of a

Task-Based Digital Library for the Academic Community, *Journal of Documentation*, **60** (4), 449–75.

Nahl, D. (2004) Measuring the Affective Information Environment of Web Searchers. In Schamber, L. and Barry, C. L. (eds), *ASIST 2004: managing and enhancing information: cultures and conflicts: proceedings of the 67th annual meeting of the American Society for Information Science & Technology*, Information Today, 191–97.

Nahl, D. (2006) Affective Load. In Fisher, K. E., Erdelez, S. and McKechnie, L. E. F. (eds), *Theories of Information Behaviour*, Information Today, 39–43.

Nicholas, D., Huntington, P., Williams, P. and Dobrowolski, T. (2004) Re-Appraising Information Seeking Behaviour in a Digital Environment: bouncers, checkers, returnees and the like, *Journal of Documentation*, **60** (1), 24–43.

Niedźwiedzka, B. (2003) A Proposed General Model of Information Behaviour, *Information Research*, **9** (1), paper 164.

Nielsen, J. and Loranger, H. (2006) *Prioritizing Web Usability*, New Riders.

Olander, B. (2007) Information Interaction Among Computer Scientists: a longitudinal study, *Information Research*, **12** (4).

Pennanen, M. and Vakkari, P. (2003) Students' Conceptual Structure, Search Process, and Outcome While Preparing a Research Proposal: a longitudinal case study, *Journal of the American Society for Information Science*, **54** (8), 759–70.

Pettigrew, K., Fidel, R. and Bruce, H. (2001) Conceptual Frameworks in Information Behaviour, *Annual Review of Information Science & Technology*, **35**, 43–78.

Pharo, N. (2004) A New Model of Information Behaviour Based on the Search Situation Transition Schema, *Information Research*, **10** (1), paper 203.

Pharo, N. and Jarvelin, K. (2004) The SST Method: a tool for analysing web information search process, *Information Processing & Management*, **40** (4), 633–54.

Ramirez, A., Walther, J. B., Burgoon, J. K. and Sunnafrank, M. (2002) Information-seeking Strategies, Uncertainty, and Computer-Mediated Communication Toward a Conceptual Model, *Human Communication Research*, **28** (2), 213–28.

Rieh, S. Y. (2002) Judgment of Information Quality and Cognitive Authority in the Web, *Journal of the American Society for Information Science and Technology*, **53** (2), 145–61.

Saracevic, T. (1997) The Stratified Model of Information Retrieval Interaction: extension and applications, *Proceedings of the American Society for Information Science*, **34**, 313–27, http://comminfo.rutgers.edu/~tefko/articles.htm.

Savolainen, R. (2007) Filtering and Withdrawing: strategies for coping with inform-ation overload in everyday contexts, *Journal of Information Science*, **33** (5), 611–21.

Savolainen, R. (2008) Source Preferences in the Context of Seeking Problem-Specific Information, *Information Processing & Management*, **44** (1), 274–93.

Savolainen, R. and Kari, J. (2006) User-Defined Relevance Criteria in Web Searching, *Journal of Documentation*, **62** (6), 685–707.

Sias, P. M. and Wyers, T. D. (2001) Employee Uncertainty and Information-Seeking in Newly-Formed Expansion Organizations, *Management Communication Quarterly*, **14**, 549–73.

Slone, D. J. (2002) The Influence of Mental Models and Goals on Search Patterns During Web Interaction, *Journal of the American Society for Information Science and Technology*, **53** (13), 1152–69.

Spink, A. (1997) Study of Interactive Feedback during Mediated Information Retrieval, *Journal of the American Society for Information Science*, **48** (5), 382–94.

Spink, A. and Cole, C. (eds) (2005) *New Directions in Human Information Behaviour*, Springer.

Spink, A. and Jansen, B. J. (2004) *Web Search: public searching of the web*, Kluwer Academic Publishers.

Spink, A., Ozmutlu, H. C. and Ozmutlu, S. (2002) Multitasking Information Seeking and Searching Processes, *Journal of the American Society for Information Science and Technology*, **53** (8), 639–52.

Tabatabai, D. and Shore, M. (2005) How Experts and Novices Search the Web, *Library & Information Science Research*, **27** (2), 222–48.

Talja, S. (2002) Information Sharing in Academic Communities: types and levels of collaboration in information seeking and use, *New Review of Information Behaviour Research*, **3**, 143–59.

Taylor, R. (1991) Information Use Environments, *Progress in Communication Science*, **10**, 217–51.

Tenopir, C., Hitchcock, B. and Pillow, A. (2003) *Use and Users of Electronic Library Resources: an overview and analysis of recent research studies*, Council on Library and Information Resources.

Tenopir, C., Brown, A., Brown, C. and Blake, C. (2006) How Chemists are Really Finding and Using Information in our Digital Environment. In *Proceedings of [the] Annual Conference of the American Society for Information Science and Technology*, www.ils.unc.edu/~cablake/Papers/Asist2006.pdf.

Thatcher, A. (2008) Web Search Strategies: the influence of web experience and task type, *Information Processing & Management*, **44** (3), 1308–29.

Vakkari, P. and Jarvelin, K. (2005) Explanation in information seeking and retrieval. In Spink, A. and Cole, C. (ed.), *New Directions in Cognitive Information Retrieval*, The Information Retrieval Series, Vol. 19, Springer, 113–38.

Wilson, T. D. (1999a), Models in Information Behaviour Research, *Journal of Documentation*, **55** (3), 249–70.

Wilson, T. D. (1999b) Exploring Models of Information Behaviour: the 'uncertainty' project. In Wilson, T. D. and Allen, D. K. (eds), *Exploring the Contexts of Information Behaviour: proceedings of the Second International Conference on Research in Information Needs, Seeking and Use in Different Contexts, 13–15 August, Sheffield*, Taylor Graham, 55–66.

Wilson, T. D. (2000) Human Information Behaviour, *Informing Science*, **3** (2), 49–55.

Wilson, T. D. (2006a) Revisiting User Studies and Information Needs, *Journal of Documentation*, **62** (6), 680–84.

Wilson, T. D. (2006b), 60 Years of the Best in Information Research on User Studies and Information Needs, *Journal of Documentation*, **62** (6), 658–70.

Wilson, T. D., Ellis, D., Ford, N. and Foster, A. (2000) Uncertainty in Information Seeking: a research project in the Department of Information Studies, http://informationr.net/tdw/publ/unis/uncerty.html.

Wilson, T. D., Ellis, D., Ford, N., Foster, A. and Spink, A. (2002) Information Seeking and mediated searching, Part 2: uncertainty and its correlates, *Journal of the American Society for Information Science and Technology*, **53** (9), 704–15.

Xu, Y. (2007) The Dynamics of Interactive Information Retrieval Behaviour, Part I: an activity theory perspective, *Journal of the American Society for Information Science and Technology*, **58** (7), 958–70.

Yovits, M. C. and Foulk, C. R. (1985) Experiments and Analysis of Information Use and Value in a Decision Making Context, *Journal of the American Society for Information Science*, **36**, 63–81.

4

Usability study basics

Introduction

As discussed in Chapter 1, usability is a quality attribute of information services and products. Usability research aims to gather data on how a particular information service or product is used and perceived by users, how far the given product or service meets its stated objectives, where users find difficulties in using the product or service, if any, and so on. Usability studies may be conducted at different stages of the lifecycle of an information product or service. At the design stage data relating to the anticipated or expected uses of a specific information service or product can be gathered through a usability study. More usability information relating to how far an information product or service meets its stated goals can be gathered after development of the prototype but before implementation. Again usability information has to be gathered at different intervals when the product is on the market in order to gather data on the usage patterns and user perceptions about the strengths and weaknesses of the given information product or service. In summary, usability studies need to be conducted throughout the lifecycle and different information is gathered to help improve the product or service and to remain effective and competitive in the marketplace. This chapter discusses the concept of usability in more detail and how to conduct a usability study at different stages of a product lifecycle, including various approaches, tools and techniques.

Usability

The definition of usability provided in ISO 9241-11:1998, mentioned in Chapter 1, emphasizes that usability is a measure of the extent to which a given product can be used by specified users to achieve some specified goals. It also reminds us that users should be able to use the given product with effectiveness, efficiency and satisfaction in a specified context of use. This definition therefore suggests that to measure usability, we need to:

- identify a subset of the specified set of users and involve them in the study, and then
- study the selected participants' context and goals for which they are going to use the product
- assess how the study participants use the information product or service to perform their tasks and accomplish their goals; it is also necessary to find out how efficiently the participants can use the various features and function of the information product or service, and what their overall perception and level satisfaction with the product or service is.

Shneiderman and Plaisant (2010, 13) stated that usability, universality and usefulness can be achieved by 'thoughtful planning, sensitivity to user needs, devotion to requirements analysis, and diligent testing'.

While usability is an important feature of an information product or service, another associated characteristic is utility. After all, an information product or service need not only be easy to use, but it should also be useful – it should meet certain utility or usability criteria. For example, a website may be easy to use but it may not contain all the necessary information that users need to perform a task within a specific context. It should be remembered that people do not use an information product or service out of intrinsic enjoyment of such activities but because they want to do something else – they have a job to do, a task to complete, a problem to solve – or at least have cognitive needs such as to reach a level of mental satisfaction by knowing or reading something. Therefore, an information product or service should be useful in helping people performing their tasks or accomplishing their goals. However, an online information product or service should have certain attributes in order to reduce the burden on users while using the product or service. Nielsen and Loranger (2006) suggest that usability has five attributes, which in an online information product or service are:

- *Learnability*: How easily can users accomplish basic tasks the first time they encounter a specific information service or product? For instance, can all the features and functions be used by new and novice users effectively?

- *Efficiency*: How quickly can users accomplish the tasks they are expected to perform with a given information product or service? For instance, how quickly can users identify the specific features and functions of the product or service in order to gather the information they need to accomplish a task?
- *Memorability*: How easily can users memorize the different activities required to use a specific information product or service, and how easily can they re-establish proficiency when they come back after some time? For instance, does the product or service use terms, phrases, symbols and design features that are suitable for the target users and their context, and does the site use them consistently?
- *Likelihood of errors*: How error prone is the system, and how easily can users recover from an error? For instance, how often does the system produce errors? There should be as few errors as possible, and when they occur the system should come up with an appropriate error message and indicate a recovery path.
- *Satisfaction*: How satisfied are users with the given information product or service? For instance, what are the general user perceptions about the quality and uniqueness of the product or service and how do the features and facilities compare with other competitive products on the market, if any?

It may be noted that many, if not all, of the usability attributes described above depend as much on the specific design of the information product or service as they do on users themselves and a host of other contextual and environmental factors. In other words, usability attributes are not fixed for all users; a given information product or service may be highly usable for a given user or a community, but it may not be the same for others.

A usability study may be conducted to assess an entire information product or service with reference to all its features and functionalities, or it may be conducted to assess one or more of its specific features. Alternatively a usability study may be conducted to compare various information products and services or comparable features of some selected information products and services, for example only the search interface and search options of comparable products as opposed to every feature and functionality. Whatever approach is taken, the overall goal of a usability study is always to improve the quality and efficiency of the information product or service and thus to meet the user requirements in a better way.

Factors affecting usability

Usability of information products and services depend on a number of factors ranging from the nature, volume and characteristics of the content or product, coupled with a variety of user-related factors such as the user's age and gender, abilities, backgrounds, motivations, personalities, cultures, work environment, work lifestyles, ICT and information skills, accessibility to ICT and the web, and so on. It is therefore extremely difficult, if not impossible, to design information products and services that will meet the usability requirements for every user in every part of the world. Yet, with the availability and growth of the web, there is a growing expectation among businesses and users that every system can and should be used by everyone with equal ease and level of satisfaction. Inclusion rather than exclusion for every digital information product and service has been the aim of every government, industry and institution. A government information service on policies, health or education aims to reach out to every member of a country. Similarly digital information products and services provided by universities, health authorities or financial institutions aim to meet the requirements of all categories of users in a given country, or, in most cases, anywhere in the world.

This raises significant challenges not only to the designers of information products and services but also to the service providers. Usability studies can play a major role and help designers and service providers by advising them what users need, how they can and cannot use some aspects of the given information product or service, what can be done to improve the product or service, and so on. Barriers to digital information access and use that in turn affect the usability of information products and services are discussed in Chapter 9.

How to conduct a usability study

Designing a usability study needs careful planning and execution, and most importantly a clear understanding of the product or service that is being studied and the type of users who would participate in the study. A variety of design and usability guidelines are available in literature, for example,

Shneiderman and Plaisant (2010) provided detailed guidelines for designing usable user interfaces, while other researchers like Nielsen and Loranger (2006), Pearrow (2007) and Spiliotopoulos el al. (2010) discussed usability guidelines for websites. A number of other excellent sources giving guidelines for usability studies include Kuniavsky (2003), Rubin and Chisnell (2008), Tullis and Albert (2008) and Albert, Tullis and Tedesco (2010).

Kuniavsky (2003) suggested four major steps for usability testing:

• Define users and their goals.
• Create tasks that address those goals.
• Get the right people.
• Watch them try to perform the tasks.

Although these are the essential steps in a usability test, the above list does not include key steps that form the foundation of any usability study such as planning the test, creating the study objectives and research questions, and determining the study methods and locations or settings.

Rubin and Chisnell (2008) listed the following basic elements of usability testing:

• development of research questions or test objectives
• use of a representative sample of end users as study participants
• representation of the actual work environment
• observation of study participants using the product under study
• interviewing of the participants
• collection of quantitative and qualitative measures
• recommendation of necessary improvements.

While these are useful, and more comprehensive guidelines than those provided by Kuniavsky (discussed above), they limit the study and data collection methods to observation and interviews, while in reality a variety of other methods may be employed depending on the design and objectives of the usability study.

Based on the guidelines suggested by various researchers the following general guidelines are proposed for conducting usability studies of information products and services:

• Plan a usability study: develop test objectives and research questions.

- Choose usability metrics and data collection methods.
- Select study participants.
- Conduct the tests and collect data.
- Analyse data and make recommendations.

Planning a usability study

First, it is important to decide the goals of the usability study. The most important question at this stage is to decide exactly what is to be measured or assessed. A user study may be designed to gather information about:

- the overall features of an information product or service
- specific features or aspects of an information product or service
- a new functionality of an information product or service
- success rates, task completion rates and so on
- user behaviour, activities and/or performance with reference to a specific information product or service
- overall user satisfaction with a specific information product or service
- comparison of similar or competitive information products or services
- the sustainability of an information product or service.

Once the overall goal of a usability study is determined, it is important to prepare a list of research questions that a usability study should aim to answer. These questions will be helpful in the overall planning, which should take into account factors such as:

- the overall goals of the specific product or service
- the specific features or issues to be studied about the study participants
- metrics and methods for collection
- analysis of data
- the amount of the budget
- the time for conducting the usability study.

While the type of usability study has to be decided by its overall objectives (the product or service that is going to be evaluated and the study participants who would evaluate the product or service), a number of management issues also have to be considered, the most obvious of which relates to the budget and timeline affecting the design, scope and implementation of the project. Thus the evaluation goals, methods, metrics, participants, study team (evaluators or moderators) and overall process depend entirely on the study's costs and time constraints. The cost and time for conducting usability studies increases significantly as researchers move from the design stage to the implementation and operation stage. Cost and study time also depend significantly on the methods and metrics used, the number of study participants, study locations and so on. Costs may be budgeted for within the lifecycle of an information product or service. For example, a separate research budget was approved for conducting the usability study of the Europeana Digital Library (discussed in Chapter 8). However, in many cases usability studies form part of regular software research development activities and are carried out regularly by commercial search service providers, database and journal aggregator services and so on. In order for an information product or service to be innovative, usable and better than its competitors, regular usability studies are essential and the costs for such studies should be built into the product design and lifecycle.

Choosing usability metrics

As discussed earlier in this chapter, five characteristics of the usability of an information product or service can be measured: learnability, efficiency, memorability, likelihood of errors and satisfaction rate. It may be noted that four of these usability criteria focus primarily on system features rather than users. Ben Shneiderman (Shneiderman and Plaisant, 2010), the guru of interface design, proposed there are eight golden rules of user interface design:

- Strive for consistency.
- Cater to universal usability.
- Offer informative feedback.
- Design dialogues to yield closure.
- Prevent errors.
- Permit easy reversal of actions.
- Support internal locus of control.
- Reduce short-term memory load.

Although this is only one component of usability, the rules also play a key role in improving the overall usability of information products and services.

A closer look at these rules shows they are critical for the success of an information product and service because the user interface is the first and last port of call for a user to get access to and use an information product or service. Consequently the user interface should achieve all the usability goals, thereby facilitating access to and use of the product or service behind it. Furthermore, Shneiderman's second rule ('Cater to universal usability') specifically advocates that user studies should be designed to take into account diverse user categories, such as novice and expert users and users of different ages, genders and technological ability. Therefore, although created specifically for interface design, Shneiderman's metrics also determine the usability of the resulting information product or service. However, these metrics do not specifically mention those factors that need to be considered in relation to a specific task or the overall utility and user satisfaction in relation to a specific information product or service. Fortunately there are other usability standards and guidelines that cover these issues, which are discussed below.

The Common Industry Format (CIF) standard (ANSI NCITS 354-2001) prescribes a set of three usability metrics that are more detailed and relate to specific users tasks, success rates, efficiency and user satisfaction (Pearrow, 2007):

- *effectiveness*, which can be measured by such factors as the percentage of tasks completed, ratio of success to failures, number of features or commands used and overall workload
- *efficiency*, which can be measured by such factors as the time taken to complete a task, time taken to learn to use the product or service, time spent on errors, number or percentages of errors, frequency of use of help, and number of repeated or failed commands
- *satisfaction*, which can be measured by using rating scales for measuring the usefulness of a product or service, rating scales for measuring the satisfaction with specific features or functions, by counting the number of times the user gets upset or frustrated, and users' overall perception of the information service or product in relation to performing a specific task or solving problems.

It may be noted that a given usability study need not measure all of these factors and also any combination of them can form part of a usability study. As discussed in Chapter 2 and later in the book (Chapter 6), depending on the research method and data collection tools, quantitative measures of these factors can be generated to produce specific or comparable data for particular functionalities, products or services, or can generate comparable data for more than one service or product. It may also be argued that sometimes it is difficult to measure user satisfaction on a numeric scale and therefore the researcher may have to revert to qualitative measures and use specific user comments about specific tasks and contexts in order to make judgements.

Quantitative vs qualitative analysis

Quantitative research involves collecting numerical data that can be analysed using a number of statistical methods in order to draw conclusions that can be generalized with some degree of confidence for the entire population. Qualitative research involves collecting verbal (non-numerical) data that provides detailed information about an event or a phenomenon. In qualitative research data is collected through direct interactions between the researcher and study participants, often through interviews, observations and so on, which can be obtrusive. In quantitative research data is collected indirectly by using instruments such as questionnaires, transaction logs, automatic screen capture and mouse click software. In quantitative research data is mostly mathematical, which allows for statistical analysis and inference. In qualitative research the data is textual, gathered in the form of observation notes, interview scripts, audio or video recordings and so on; it cannot be used for statistical analysis, and needs to be interpreted with reference to the specific context and study objectives.

Quantitative research provides answers to what happens, for example about usage statistics, task completion rates, success and failure rates and so on. Thus quantitative research gives us an indication of problems, if any, and how they are related to various features and functions of an information product or service. Qualitative research provides in depth information about what the exact problems are and why, and suggests how to fix them. In user studies a combination of both types of research produces the best results, and therefore combined approaches are used in many usability studies.

Usability study methods

A variety of data collection methods and tools are used for conducting usability tests, depending on a number of factors, especially the type of usability test being conducted such as formative or summative evaluation (discussed later in this chapter), study objectives, study participants, budget and available time. Some of the most common methods are explained below.

Card sorting

As discussed earlier in this chapter, usability studies should be conducted at the early stages of product design. However, at the earliest stage of the product development lifecycle it is very difficult to conceive the nature of the information product or service to be developed let alone involve users to evaluate it. Card sorting is a fast and relatively easy technique that may be very useful at this stage. It is used to uncover how potential users categorize and organize information, and this knowledge can be used to design a usable information product or service. Card sorting provides very good insight of how users would like to see their information organized or structured and thus it can form the foundation of the design process (Pearrow, 2007). Card sorting exercises can be undertaken when the designer knows what kind of information needs to be organized, and this is usually done when the purpose, features and audience or users of an information product or service have been determined but before an architecture or design of the product has been conceived (Kuniavsky, 2003). Card sorting exercises can play a key role in determining the findability of information within an information product or service. For example, they will tell us whether the target users of an information product or service would prefer to browse or search as their mode of access to information, or whether they prefer more text or images or a combination of both on the interface.

Wireframes and paper prototyping

Paper prototypes or wireframes are paper-based designs of an information product or service that can be used to gather some usability data. Wireframes are very common tools used by designers of information products and services. Through simple line drawings, they provide a visual representation of various functionalities and workflows required of a product or service. For example, through wireframes, it may be possible to identify and create links among various specific functions and features of a product or service. This will also point out the chain of activities or mouse clicks that a user has to perform in order to move to a specific feature or functionality. Therefore wireframes provide valuable insights and identify specific design requirements. Wireframes can also be used to conduct usability tests at the very early stage of product design. The value of wireframes or paper prototypes is that some critical usability information can be gathered quickly and inexpensively with minimal resources before the product is produced.

Expert or heuristic evaluation

Expert or heuristic evaluation is one of the most cost-effective and useful tools for usability studies. As the name suggests, the evaluation is conducted by one or more experts – usually the system designers or professional experts – who investigate how a product or service meets its stated objectives, how various features and functions work and with what effects. These notes are compiled and recommendations are made for modifications or improvements. Nielsen (2003) proposed ten usability heuristics, which are widely used for conducting usability studies of website and web-based information products and services. These are discussed in Chapter 7. Sometimes walk-throughs are used as part of the heuristic evaluation where the designer guides some colleagues or experts through the actual user tasks while recording or noting the success or failure rates, difficulties encountered, if any, and so on. Instead of the designer playing the role of the user, a real user or client may be brought in to conduct walk-throughs (Rubin and Chisnell, 2008).

Participatory or user-centred design

With the mantra 'Know thy user', every usable information product or service should focus on the principles of user-centred design. As discussed in more detail in Chapter 7, participatory or user-centred design approach dictates that some end users should be involved from the very early stages of the product design and development lifecycle. User-centred design is both a 'design and a philosophy that puts the user's needs ahead of anything else' (Pearrow, 2007, 61). Several international standards, notably ISO 9241 part 11 (ISO 9241-11:1998) and ISO 9241 part 210 (ISO 9241-210:2010), prescribe guidelines for user-centred design and usability metrics. ISO 9241-210 provides guidelines for requirements and recommendations for user-centred design principles and activities that can be applied to any information product or service. Products or services can then be measured against the three main usability requirements – efficiency, effectiveness and satisfaction – prescribed by ISO 9241-11.

Ethnographic research

Ethnographic research methods are increasingly being used in qualitative research in order to gather information about users within specific contexts. They are normally used in the field of anthropology. The essence of ethnographic research is that users are studied in their normal setting, for example at their study, workplaces or home depending on the objectives and design of the usability study. By using a variety of qualitative approaches to data collection such as observation, interviews and group discussions (discussed in Chapter 2), the researcher can develop user profiles, personas, task descriptions and scenarios that can be used to design and evaluate an information product or service. As discussed later in this book (Chapter 7), many usability researchers use ethnographic research techniques for gathering usability data for digital libraries and information services.

Focus group research

Focus group research methods (discussed in Chapter 2) are one of the most commonly employed methods for data collection in qualitative research, and are consequently used widely in conducting usability studies. They can be used at the early stages of a product design to evaluate early design approaches and as 'proof of concept', when gathering data from a group of users about a product or service that is on the market, or to compare certain features of competitive products or services. Focus groups are good for gathering general qualitative information, but do not produce specific data on tasks, completion time, error rates and so on, for which other methods like surveys or log analysis are more appropriate.

Surveys

Surveys are the most commonly employed method for collecting usability data. As discussed in Chapter 2, a variety of data collection methods may be employed in surveys ranging from questionnaires to interviews, diaries, observations supported by questionnaires, interviews or think aloud and so on. Surveys can be conducted at any stage of the product lifecycle, but they are usually employed when the product or service is on the market or as a beta test just before the official launch. They are expensive and often time consuming since direct user involvement is required, and depending on the tools employed, analysis of the survey data may be labour intensive. However, surveys often produce a variety of quantitative and qualitative data about an information product or service, which can be extremely useful in making further design and/or marketing decisions.

Log analysis

Transaction log analysis (discussed in Chapter 2) is an extremely useful and relatively easy method for collecting usability data. Although it collects usage statistics, based on what is often called the digital footprints of users (Biddle, 2009), they are unobtrusive and can be conducted at any time without directly interfering with users or the information product or service concerned. Log analyses produce rich data, which combined with usability data collected through other methods like surveys and/or focus groups can be extremely useful in making design and strategic business decisions like whether or not to continue the product or service, whether or not the current marketing and/or business model is appropriate and so on. Some usability studies based on log analyses are discussed later in this book (see Chapters 7 and 8).

Selecting study participants

When conducting a usability study, researchers should keep the following questions in mind in relation to the study participants (Tullis and Albert, 2008):

- What type of participants are needed?
- How many participants are needed?
- Does the data need to be collected and compared from a single group or a number of groups of participants?
- Is it necessary to counterbalance the order of tasks in order to make sure that appropriate data is gathered from different users or groups for various activities?

The most obvious challenge when selecting participants for a usability study is to find out who uses the product or service that is going to be evaluated. This is a more difficult job than it sounds especially for the modern-day web-based information products and services like digital libraries and information services. If an information product is designed for a niche market or a specific group of users it is easy to pinpoint specific user groups. However, if an information product or service is designed for almost everyone in a country or in the world, like the United Nations Information Service (UNIS; www.unis.unvienna.org/), Europeana Digital Library (www.europeana.eu/portal/), Directgov, the UK government information service (www.direct.gov.uk/en/index.htm), American Memory (http://memory.loc.gov/ammem/index.html) or a digital library of American history from the US Library of Congress, it is difficult to select specific user groups because they may be anyone in any corner of a given country, region or the world. Selection of users for a usability study should also consider such questions as:

- What are the goals of users?
- What are the specific tasks of users that they want to accomplish by gathering information from the information product or service concerned?
- What is the overall user context, such as user characteristics, work environment, lifestyle and so on?
- How much information from the service or product do users need to accomplish their tasks – anything, something, everything?

There are detailed discussions on the criteria for selecting users for usability studies in Chapter 5.

Conducting the tests and collecting data

Usability studies may be conducted during the product development stage and when the product is on the market. Figure 4.1 shows the types of usability studies that might be used at different stages of a product development life-cycle. Two broad types of evaluation are conducted during the product development stage:

- Formative evaluation takes place throughout the design process; it is iterative, conducted by the design team or experts, sometimes with a small number of users.
- Summative evaluation is conducted when the prototype has been designed and before implementation.

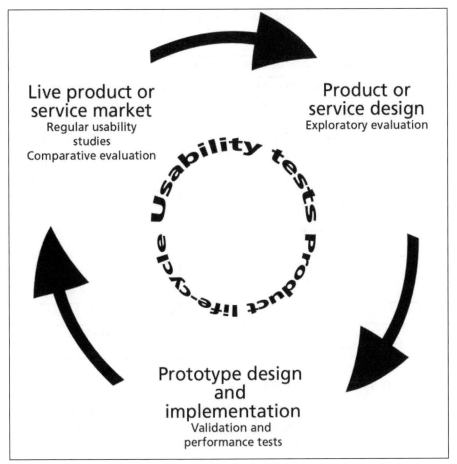

Figure 4.1 *Usability studies and the product lifecycle*

Table 4.1 (overleaf) provides a comparison of formative and summative evaluation.

Regular usability studies need to be conducted when the information product or service is in the marketplace and in operation in order to find out whether and how it meets its stated objectives vis-à-vis the user requirements, the overall objectives of the company, the overall market trends and so on. These usability studies may be conducted directly by involving users of the products and services or indirectly by analysing usage and transaction data.

Tullis and Albert (2008) identified ten different types of usability study. Choice of study depends on a number of factors ranging from the goals of the study, users or participants of the study, technology available, methods and tools used for collecting data, and resources and expertise available to conduct the study.

Table 4.1 *Formative vs summative evaluation*

Features	Formative evaluation	Summative evaluation
Objectives	Diagnosis and quick fix	Measurement
Why	In order to: • understand user problems • understand usability system problems • choose between alternative designs • develop an iterative design approach that can be checked and modified, if necessary at every stage.	To find out: • how usable the product is • whether it meets the usability requirements • whether it needs further improvement • how it compares with other products.
When	Early in design and development	After the prototype design and throughout the product development lifecycle
Outcome	Fast iteration	Major changes or redesign
How	Eliminate as many problems as possible early on	Adapt to market requirements

Comparing alternative designs

Often a usability study is designed to compare alternative designs of an information service or product. This is often done as a formative evaluation where various alternative designs are tested early on against a set of usability criteria, or through a small group of users. Generally the outcome of such usability studies is a set of points highlighting the strengths and weaknesses of each design or a set of comparative statistics or figures that are used to choose one specific design over another.

Comparing products

Sometimes usability studies are conducted to compare specific features or strengths and weaknesses between competing products or services. These can be carried out when more than one competing product or service is available, and the researcher wants to compare them against a set of benchmarks or criteria. Often such studies are designed around measuring three sets of features:

- *task completion rate*: how many users can complete specific tasks
- *efficiency*: how quickly and effortlessly users can accomplish their tasks using the service or product
- *overall user satisfaction* with the information product or service.

Completing a transaction

Often a usability study focuses on completing a specific transaction, for example completing a search process using a particular information product or service. Such studies should aim to measure the success rates among a set of users, for example between the groups of expert and novice users, students and researchers, or male and female users, and so on. Sometimes effectiveness of the information product or service is also measured and thereby specific problems, if any, are identified relating to specific user tasks and activities.

Evaluating frequent use of the same product

Sometimes an information product or service, for example a digital book, is meant to be used frequently. In such cases it is important to measure certain specific usability metrics like the time taken to accomplish a specific task, learnability and memorability of specific features or activities associated with the product or service.

Evaluating navigation and/or information architecture

Sometimes usability studies are conducted to test the navigation features or information architecture of an information product or service with a view to finding out how users can find the required information by moving between various options or links, how they know where they are and how to go somewhere from there. Typically this kind of usability is conducted at the design stage by using wireframes or with a prototype where users are asked to perform a set of tasks. Card sorting may be used for initial design of navigation and information architecture for an information product or service, as it would tell how a potential group of users would like to organize the information they need for some tasks or activities.

Increasing awareness

Some usability studies are conducted to gather data on user awareness of the specific feature(s) of a product or service. By monitoring user interactions directly by using some kind of software that captures this, or through log analysis, it may be possible to identify to what extent users are aware of the various functionalities of an information product or service. For example, a usability study may be designed to see whether users are aware of the features of Google Books or Google Scholar, telling them whether or not the retrieved book or article is available in their local library.

Discovering problems

Most usability studies aim to find out not only what the strengths of a product or service are, but also what the weaknesses are and what typical problems users face, and which features really annoy users, force them to abandon an operation, and so on. Such usability studies should be conducted at all levels – with all categories of users, and with every function or feature of the service – and should be conducted regularly in order to minimize the problems and weaknesses of an information product or service. Issues-based metrics may be appropriate for problem discovery, as even though the exact problems facing each individual study participant may be different, together they provide a clear picture of the problems associated with certain issues (Tullis and Albert, 2008).

Maximizing usability of a critical product

Some products or services are designed to be used regularly while others are produced for use in accomplishing critical activities such as online voting or payments and transactions. For such products or services, it is important to measure task success with as many users and specific tasks as possible in order to minimize errors and maximize success rates. Success rate is much more important in such cases than overall user satisfaction – how users feel about the product or service.

Evaluating the impact of subtle changes

Subtle changes such as changes in the visual design, colour, font size or reordering of options may have a huge impact on the usability of an information product or service. Perhaps these sorts of design changes should be tested at the very early stage with alternative designs in order to measure their potential impact on users and the overall usability of the product or service. With live online products, such tests may be conducted by diverting users to an alternative page to perform certain tasks with the new design features, which can be compared with similar data generated for the user activities on the usual site or product.

Creating a positive user experience

An information product or service should not only be usable, but create a good impression on users, which will attract them in future. It is therefore important to find out what the user actually feels about the product or service. Several direct and indirect metrics may be used; for example, the user may be asked to use a scale to show their level of satisfaction, appreciation and so on, or they may be asked indirect questions like whether they would like to recommend the given product or service to their friends and colleagues.

It may be noted that normally a usability study would like to measure a number of features or aspects of an information product or service and therefore a combination of the above types of studies may have to be undertaken.

Project management issues

Objectives and type of usability study and the corresponding methods for each should be considered in association with some critical management issues. Depending on the nature of the information product or service, the user market and study participants, a user study can be expensive and time consuming. Hence budget and time constraints are the two major project management issues that need to be considered at the very early stages of a usability study. Other important factors are the characteristics and goals of the parent organization providing the information product or service. For example, the goals of the Europeana Digital Library (www.europeana.eu), which aims to provide one-stop access to Europe's cultutural heritage information (discussed in Chapter 8), are quite different from those of Directgov (www.direct.gov.uk), an online service that makes available a variety of information about UK government services, regulations and practices for UK residents and citizens. Decisions must also be made at the start of a usability study about the number of researchers or staff needed to conduct the study, their experience and expertise.

Labs vs user sites

Usability tests can be conducted in a typical lab environment, or at user sites. Again, the researcher needs to decide whether the tests have to be conducted in one or multiple locations. Often it is not an easy decision to make a choice between these two options, and yet the outcomes of the study may be significantly influenced by the choice made. While there is no easy answer to this question, and both sites have advantages and disadvantages, answers to the following questions may help the researcher make an appropriate decision:

- What are the overall objectives of the usability study and is it necessary that users need to be studied in their workplace or normal life settings?
- Who are the users (potential study participants), how many of them are there and where are they located?
- Will users' normal workplace environment have any positive or negative influence on the outcomes of the study?
- Does the study need to use any special equipments or tools, such as a video camera or special software to capture user activities online? If so, how easy or difficult will it be to install and use such devices at users' workplaces?
- Is the usability study designed to be obtrusive or unobtrusive? Is it important that the researcher is present at the time of the study and is this likely to have any impact on its outcomes?
- How many participants are required or expected to take part at one time and what data collection method is being used?
- Can users come to the lab site easily, with minimum effort, cost, time?
- Are participants being paid to take part in the test? Some researchers feel that payment mechanisms in any form may act as an incentive for participants who may not be the most appropriate, and this may affect the overall results of the study.
- Will the somewhat artificial environment of the lab affect the study outcomes? Will participants, for example young children, members of a specific gender or ethnic community and so on, feel uncomfortable or

threatened in any way within the lab setting?

- Does the study need to be carried out simultaneously with many users and/or at many locations?
- Is the context of one user group different from another and will this context be better captured while studying users in their own environment?
- Are there any time constraints and will this have any impact on the choice of study locations?
- Is it possible to get permission to run the tests at users' workplaces?
- Will the typical lab setting involve a number of users using the same information product or service at the same time, and will there be any differences if users are studied while they are using the same information product or service alone?
- Can the external factors be controlled within a user's workplace that might affect the outcomes of the study?

A careful thinking process and answers to the above questions will lead the researcher towards the right direction for choosing the better alternative between lab and site testing, and between single and multiple site testing.

Analysing data

Depending on its nature and design a usability study may produce a variety of quantitative and qualitative data. This data needs to be analysed in the light of the research questions and the study objectives in order to be able to draw some useful conclusions that may then be used to prepare a set of recommendations for improvement of the given information product or service. Chapter 6 discusses some of the basic approaches to analysis of data from usability studies.

Summary

Some basics of usability studies are discussed in this chapter. Usability studies can be conducted at any stage of a product development cycle – during the design process, after developing the prototype and before implementation, and when the product is operating on the market. However, a usability study depends on a number of factors, such as the nature of the information product or service, users, objectives of the usability study, availability of resources and time. Various usability guidelines, including some international standards, are available, and a researcher can choose and use a variety of usability metrics. Usability studies can be conducted with minimum user involvement at the early stages of design or through heuristic (expert) evaluation, and by involving a number of participants or user groups, in one or more study locations, and in lab or real life settings.

Similarly a variety of data collection methods can be employed, some of which may generate qualitative data while others may produce quantitative and measurable statistics; both are important in producing usability figures and findings. Success of a usability study depends significantly on proper and careful planning, the selection of study participants, and appropriate study methods and data collection tools and techniques. Data may be collected through direct or indirect involvements or participation of users, and appropriate research ethics guidelines should be followed and appropriate clearance should be obtained when direct user participation is expected. Sometimes indirect methods like transaction log analysis can produce some valuable and rich data, but a combination of direct and indirect data collection methods and appropriate qualitative and quantitative approaches produces the best results.

References

Albert, B., Tullis, T. and Tedesco, T. (2010) *Beyond the Usability Lab: conducting large-scale online user experience studies*, Morgan Kaufmann.

ANSI NCITS 354-2001 *Common Industry Format for Usability Test Reports*, American National Standards Institution.

Biddle, D. (2009) Rushes Sequences, David Nicholas interview - London (Video), BBC, Monday 7 Dec. 2009, www.bbc.co.uk/blogs/digitalrevolution/2009/12/rushes-sequences-david-nichola.shtml.

ISO 9241-11:1998 *Ergonomic Requirements for Office Work with Visual Display Terminals (VDTs), Part 11: guidance on usability*, International Organization for Standardization.

ISO 9241-210:2010 *Ergonomics of Human-System Interaction, Part 210: human-centred design for interactive systems*, International Organization for Standardization.

Kuniavsky, M. (2003) *Observing the User Experience: a practitioner's experience to user research*, Morgan Kaufmann.

Nielsen, J. (2003) *Usability 101: introduction to usability*, www.useit.com/alertbox/20030825.html.

Nielsen, J. and Loranger, H. (2006) *Prioritizing Web Usability*, New Riders.

Pearrow, M. (2007) *Web Usability Handbook*, 2nd edn, Charles River Media.

Rubin, J. and Chisnell, D. (2008) *Handbook of Usability Testing: how to plan, design and conduct effective tests*, Wiley Publishing.

Shneiderman, B. and Plaisant, C. (2010) *Designing the User Interface: strategies for effective human-computer interaction*, 5th edn, Addison-Wesley.

Spiliotopoulos, T., Papadopoulou, P., Martakos, D. and Kouroupetroglou, G. (eds) (2010) *Integrating Usability Engineering for Designing the Web Experience: methodologies and principles*, Information Science Reference.

Tullis, T. and Albert, B. (2008) *Measuring the User Experience: collecting, analyzing and presenting usability metrics*, Morgan Kaufmann.

5

Usability study participants

Introduction

As discussed in Chapter 4, the success of a usability study depends significantly on the selection of appropriate study participants. Sometimes it is not easy to identify who the actual and potential users of an information product or service are, and this makes the job of selecting participants for a usability study even more difficult. However, combining the most suitable groups of study participants and the most appropriate data collection methods can produce the best results in a usability study. This chapter discusses some basic issues related to the selection of participants for usability studies of information products and services. It also discusses various techniques for user sampling and the ethical requirements associated with the selection of study participants and usability studies in general.

Selection of study participants

An information product or service is designed to meet the information requirements of a group of users. Depending on the nature and content of the specific information product or service, sometimes these users can be very specific, for example, a group of scientists, professionals or researchers, or members of the general public. Nonetheless, the overall goal of a usability study is to assess how far the given information product or service achieves its stated objectives of meeting the information needs of the target users. Hence knowing who the target users are of an information product or service is the first step in conducting a usability study.

Creating a user profile

Before designing an information product or service, it is important to identify the potential users, record their information behaviour, and find out the tasks or activities for which they would need to use the information product or service. This information is used to create a user profile, which forms the basis of the design. This information can also be used at a later stage of the product lifecycle in order to conduct usability testing.

Usually a user profile is created at the very early stages of a product development. This is dictated by the business and goals of the organization that is developing an information product or service, the nature of the product, the specific objective and goals of the product, the target users, and the specific tasks or activities for which they would need the new or modified information product or service. These user profiles often change as the given information product or service progresses through several design and development lifecycles. Consequently, often when an information product or service is on the market for some time it is very difficult to find the initial or original user profiles used to design the original product or service. Furthermore, when a completely new information product or service is designed, especially in course of a research study, it may be difficult to identify and involve the target and potential users. Often therefore the initial design tasks begin with scenarios and personas that are a paper-based representation of a typical user world, their tasks in meeting information needs, and so on.

Often an information product or service is designed to cater for different user categories and user markets. In such cases, many user profiles are created at the design stages, which can be used for usability testing. However, as mentioned in the previous paragraph, often the original user profiles get buried under several project documentation papers, especially when the product goes through several design changes. In some cases, user information is rarely collected systematically or recorded for future reference. Often researchers investigating a new information product or service design begin with a very broad or vague idea about user requirements and behaviour, and the design team or the business concerned depend on their intuition and generic market analysis reports. Clear delineation of user characteristics often leads to failure of the information product or service, because without a clear knowledge and understanding of users and their specific characteristics and tasks it is very difficult to create a consistent and well designed product or service that can help users accomplish their tasks effectively and efficiently.

This kind of problem was faced in the course of the usability study of the SCRAN digital library service conducted by one of the authors of this book a few years ago. In order to build the user profiles that had formed the bases of the SCRAN service the usability study team had to conduct a series of discussion sessions with the service design and management team and then analyse minutes of meetings, the original funding proposal and the business plan (Chowdhury, McMenemy and Poulter, 2008, 2006a, 2006b). These studies helped the usability research team develop an idea of the target users of the product, which in turn helped them select the usability study participants.

A completely different kind of problem was faced by the other author of this book in the course of the usability study of a new information product for the EU funded research project REVEAL THIS. Since the information product was being developed as a new and innovative information service, compared with those available on the market at that time, some form of scenario-based evaluation had to be undertaken to generate usability data (Chowdhury and Landoni, 2006).

From the above two anecdotes it is clear that often very useful information about the potential market and users is stored in project and design documentation, and often for new and innovative products, user scenarios are created that are used to conduct usability studies. Information required for generating a user profile may be obtained from a variety of sources, such as:

- *market intelligence*, providing some information about the potential marketplace, competitors, functionalities and failures of the competing information products or services
- *business plan and management decisions*, specifying the business plan that formed the basis of the management decision to initiate or launch the new project leading to the design and development of a new or revised information product or service
- *a functional specification*, a blueprint for the information product or service that describes the intended functionality of the user tasks or activities for which the functionalities would be used
- *research papers and business analysis reports*, often providing market trends and showing the growth and/or market potential in the light of various socio-economic, political and technological factors.

Issues to consider when choosing usability study participants

Conducting usability studies is often a very resource intensive task, especially for generic information products or services – those information products or services that aim to meet the information needs of a large variety of user groups and so on. Often finding the right kind and number of study participants is also a big challenge. Selection of study participants depends on a number of factors, which are discussed below.

The kind of usability study being conducted

The most important determining factor is the kind of information product or service being studied, which will in turn determine the objectives of the usability study. Selection of study participants is governed by the study objective(s), for example, whether the researcher intends to gather data on the overall satisfaction of users, strengths and weaknesses of specific functionalities and so on, to compare similar information products or services, or to assess specific features such as task completion and error rates of a new or existing information product or service among the same or different categories of users.

Qualitative vs quantitative studies

What kind of approach is going to be taken and what kind of data is expected – qualitative or quantitative? In a qualitative study the number of study participants is significantly smaller than in a quantitative study. However, in the qualitative approach, more direct contact and interactions are expected to take place between the study participants and the researcher, and often the participant is expected to spend more time on the study.

Same or different types or categories of users

Depending on the nature of the usability study, the researcher needs to decide whether the same or different categories of users are to be involved. For example, for an evaluation and usability study of the Europeana Digital Library, which is designed for all categories of users, it was necessary to include different categories of users (Dobreva and Chowdhury, 2010; Skykes et al., 2010). On the other hand for the JISC national eBook observatory project (www.jiscebooksproject.org/), the study participants for the e-book service were university students (JISC, 2009; Nicholas, Rowlands and Jamali, 2010). In order to generate comparative data among disciplines, students from four different disciplines – business and management studies, engineering, medicine and media studies – were chosen.

One-off, repeated or longitudinal studies

The number of study participants also depends on whether a one-off usability study is conducted or whether a longitudinal study is conducted over a period of time at intervals in order to generate comparable data. For example, a researcher may decide to study how a particular digital library or e-book service is used by university students at different times of an academic year. In such cases, the number of study participants has to be small in order to be manageable, and the study participants should be available (for study) at different times – for example, at the beginning of the academic year, before and after the examinations and so on.

Lab-based or field studies, and number of study locations

Selection of study participants also depends on whether the usability study is being conducted in a lab or in the field at the specific user (study, home, work) locations. If the usability study is to be conducted in a lab, with especially set up equipment, then the number of study participants has to be small because only a small number of participants can be accommodated on a specific day. Alternatively, if the study is conducted simultaneously at different locations, and more importantly at the participants' usual home, study or workplace, then a number of studies can be conducted at the same time, and thus a number of participants can be involved.

How many researchers and moderators are available

Inclusion of more study participants requires more researchers and moderators to conduct, analyse and interpret the data collected in the usability study.

Researchers in usability and evaluation studies of information products and services have traditionally used quantitative methods to collect data in order to generate statistically significant results. More recently qualitative approaches have been used, where the objectives of the studies were not only to know what's happening, but why and how people use some information products and services, and thus to generate context-specific usability data. Some researchers have used a combination of qualitative and quantitative techniques in order to generate statistically significant and context-specific usability information.

User sampling

One of the main objectives of quantitative approaches to research is to generate results that are statistically significant and at the same time can be generalized. Consequently study participants for such usability and evaluation studies should be representative of the user population so the findings can be used to draw conclusions that are applicable to the wider user community.

Therefore sampling of users is an important factor for conducing usability studies. Questions that a researcher often faces in deciding the number or composition of the study participants include:

- How many study participants?
- Same or different categories of participants?
- What will be a reliable number given the study methods and level of significance?
- How to characterize each group of study participants?
- How to compare results given the composition of various study groups?

Since quantitative studies generate statistical data that needs to be interpreted in the light of the study population, it is extremely important that appropriate sampling methods are used to select study participants. A variety of sampling methods are available and the researcher needs to weigh their merits and demerits in the light of the information product or service being evaluated, the study objectives and expected outcomes. The sample study population ideally represents the entire target population, and in order to be representative, that sample must have the characteristics of the target population (Covey, 2002).

Although a usability study should maintain the anonymity of the study participants, demographic and other unique characteristics of the study population need to be clearly identified and reported in order to analyse and interpret the findings appropriately. For example, in order to conduct the usability study of some selected online health information services, a research project conducted by one of the authors of this book, it was necessary to select study participants who would be representative of the typical users of the sites, which could be virtually anyone. However, since one of the objectives of the usability study was to compare the usability features between two different sets of users – those who are well versed with modern information and communication technologies (ICTs) and a cross-section of the general public who have varying degrees of ICT skills. As a result, two different categories of study participants were chosen – a group of university students with proven ICT skills, and a group of public library users chosen randomly, representing a user population with varying degrees of ICT skills (Harbour and Chowdhury, 2007).

A variety of sampling techniques are outlined in books on research methods; see for example Denscombe (2005), Moore (2006), Pickard (2007) and Leedy and Ormrod (2009). Sampling techniques can be divided into two main categories: probability and non-probability sampling.

In probability sampling the researcher uses a statistical measure to select study population and it is possible to specify in advance that each segment of the population will be represented in the sample (Leedy and Ormrod, 2009). This is ensured by the random sampling method used in choosing the sample from the overall population. The process of selecting study subjects at random, where everyone in the target population has the same probability of being selected, is called random sampling (Covey, 2002).

In non-probability sampling it is not possible to forecast, estimate or guarantee that each element of the population will be represented in the sample (Leedy and Ormrod, 2009). There are two types of non-probability sampling: convenience sampling and quota sampling.

Random sampling

Randomization is a technique used to select study participants in such a way that the characteristics of each unit of the sample approximates to the characteristics of the total population. In this process, any member of the whole population will have an equal chance of being selected. There are many methods for random selection of a study population.

Perhaps the most frequently used method for random selection of a sample is to create a table of random numbers. In this process the study population is converted into numbers in a table in no particular order. If there is a total study population of 10,000, say, then a computer program like Microsoft Excel can be used to generate random numbers, which can be used to pick study samples from the list. A simpler approach could be to use a lottery method where every member of the population has an equal chance of being selected. For example, a unique number or details of every member of the study population may be written on a slip. Subsequently, all the slips may be put in a basket and the slips may be picked from the basket – one or many at a time – until the desired number of sample population is reached.

Systematic sampling is a variant of random sampling where some kind of control is introduced in the selection process. For example, after all members of the total population are entered in a list, in no particular order, the researcher may decide to select every n-th member (every tenth or hundredth, for example) from the list. Sometimes a random sampling technique is used to select study population from different strata of users, for example, participants from different age groups or categories – students, academics, housewives and so on. In such cases the same principle of random selection is applied to each stratum. A similar approach may be taken for selection of participants based on clusters in which case the sampling is called cluster sampling. Clusters can be identified based on geographic locations, participants' skills and experience and so on. Whichever way the sample is chosen, the essence of randomness should be maintained: any member of the population should have an equal chance of being selected.

Convenience sampling

As the name suggests this sampling technique is used as a convenience to the researcher, and consequently it is not governed by any strict statistical measures. In this method, instead of using a strict statistical approach, the researcher chooses a sampling technique that is convenient to them. As a result, the findings of the usability research cannot be generalized to a larger population because the sample study participants do not represent any defined population. Convenience sampling is used in many usability studies in order to select study participants who are easy to access and manage, and therefore it becomes easy to gather the required research data. For example, in order to study the usability of information services or products researchers select university students, in many cases students of information studies, because they are easy to reach, and running the overall usability or evaluation study becomes lot easier. Although it is easy to gather data using convenience sampling, the findings cannot be generalized because the study population does not necessarily represent the overall user population.

Quota sampling

Quota sampling is a variant of convenience sampling, where information about selected characteristics of the target population is used to select a sample set of participants. 'How well quota samples represent the target population and the accuracy of generalizations from quota sample studies depends on the accuracy of the information about the population used to establish the quota' (Covey, 2002). Quota sampling is often used by researchers because it allows them to select the right kind of study participants and therefore it becomes easy to gather the usability and evaluation data for information products and services, but because of the nature of the sampling technique, it is difficult to generalize the results for the entire population.

Purposive sampling

Sometimes the researcher chooses to select study participants from a population on the basis of the prior knowledge and understanding of the field of study and the study population. This is called purposive sampling. In this sampling method, the researcher chooses study participants in accordance with the study objectives, the domain and study context, without following any specific statistical sampling technique. As the name suggests, this kind of sampling meets the needs of the research fairly well, but there is no way to verify that the sample actually represents the characteristics of the target population. For example, for assessing the usability of a library website, an online database or a digital library, a researcher may choose a group of students from their own class or university, which may be appropriate for obtaining the required usability information. However, given the method of choosing the study sample, the research findings cannot be generalized with confidence.

Snowball sampling

Instead of choosing a set of study population based on statistical or other methods, a researcher may identify a few subjects who have the characteristics of the target population, then ask them to name other possible study participants; this process continues until the researcher gets the required data, and is called snowball sampling. It is easy to select participants and collect data in this way because the researcher only selects those participants who have the necessary characteristics of the target population and therefore are the most likely candidates for the usability and evaluation study. This method suffers from two major shortcomings: it is not possible to prove that the study sample is representative of the total population, and it allows the researcher to gather data only from users of the system or product being studied; non-users are left out because they are not selected by the researcher nor usually recommended by the selected participants.

Challenges when selecting study participants

Despite the best efforts of the researchers, recruitment of participants for usability and evaluation studies is a difficult and time consuming task. On many occasions selected study participants do not want to take part in the study voluntarily for lack of time or other reasons. As a result, increasingly several direct or indirect payments or incentives are offered to attract study participants. Making payments to research participants in the field of medical and health research is an established practice, but payments and incentives are becoming common in other fields, including information research. Sometimes study participants are also given food and/or drinks, or provided with a reward through lotteries.

While giving incentives to study participants raises the question of reliability of data, lack of a representative sample also raises questions about the reliability and validity of data. Many researchers face this dilemma because adopting appropriate sampling techniques and recruiting more study participants not only increases the reliability of the data, but also increases diversity and therefore helps achieve better research results.

In addition to the above mentioned challenges associated with the selection of study participants, such as selection of the right number and category of study participants appropriate for the nature and objectives of the usability and evaluation research, researchers often find it difficult to secure approval of the right authorities for conducting research with human subjects. Like any other research, ethical requirements require that usability and evaluation research must respect the dignity, privacy, rights and welfare of human subjects. The issues become more challenging when usability research deals with sensitive information, for example health related issues, or the study involves participants who are vulnerable, for example young children. In academic and scholarly research, universities and research institutions have developed ethical guidelines, and researchers must follow appropriate procedures in order to secure approval for research, especially when human subjects are involved. Depending on the nature of the research and study participants, the researcher is required to ensure that the anonymity, privacy and rights of the human subjects are protected throughout the research process. Often the researcher is required also to provide details of the data collection methods and instruments to be used, and other information about the nature of data to be collected, and the type of questions that will be asked. These details are checked and verified by a panel of experts or an ethics committee to ensure that appropriate ethical guidelines are being followed for the research.

Often securing such permission is a lengthy process, and therefore researchers of usability studies are required to prepare in advance. One of the major requirements of research funding bodies is that the research ethics guidelines are clearly laid out, and that appropriate mechanisms are in place (for example within the researcher's institution) to ensure they are followed by researchers. In order to secure the necessary ethics approval, researchers usually need to provide information on:

- the nature and purpose of the research
- research methods and data collection instruments
- the nature and characteristics of the study participants
- potential risks and benefits to the research subjects
- how the privacy and anonymity of research subjects will be preserved
- how the data will be analysed and applied
- how, where and for how long the data will be stored
- who will conduct the research, and what their affiliation, credentials or training are
- who will have access to the data and in what form
- the voluntary nature of the research, including a statement that data would be used only for the stated research purpose(s).

Summary

Success of usability research depends significantly on the selection of appropriate study participants. Consequently usability researchers need to consider a variety of issues. It is not possible to engage the entire study population in a usability study so an appropriate sampling technique has to be adopted. A variety of sampling techniques are available, and although adoption of an appropriate statistical probability measure for sampling study participants produces more reliable results, often researchers are required to choose non-probability sampling methods in order to make the research more manageable and to produce suitable data. Whichever method is adopted, researchers must ensure that the required ethical guidelines set up by institutions and/or research funding bodies are adhered to in order to ensure that the dignity, privacy and rights of the human subjects are properly preserved, and the data generated through the usability study is analysed and used appropriately in accordance with the stated objectives of the research.

References

Chowdhury, G., McMenemy, D. and Poulter, A. (2006a) Digital Library Evaluation: how to assess value for money? In *International Conference on Digital Libraries, Information Management for Global Access*, New Delhi, 5–8 December.

Chowdhury, G., McMenemy, D. and Poulter, A. (2006b) Large-Scale Impact of Digital Library Services: findings from a major evaluation of SCRAN. In *Research and Advanced Technology for Digital Libraries*, Lecture Notes in Computer Science, Springer, 256–66.

Chowdhury, G., McMenemy, D. and Poulter, A. (2008) MEDLIS: Model for Evaluation of Digital Libraries and Information Services, *World Digital Libraries*, **1** (1), 35–46.

Chowdhury, S. and Landoni, M. (2006) News Aggregator Services: user expectations and experience, *Online Information Review*, **30** (2), 2006, 100–15.

Covey, D. T. (2002) Usage and Usability Assessment: library practices and concerns, CLIR Report 105, Digital Library Federation, Council on Library and Information Resources, www.clir.org/pubs/reports/pub105/pub105.pdf.

Denscombe, M. (2005) *The Good Research Guide: for small-scale social research projects*, 2nd edn, Open University Press.

Dobreva, M. and Chowdhury, S. (2010) A User-Centric Evaluation of the Europeana Digital Library. In *International Conference on Asia-Pacific Digital Libraries*, 148–57.

Harbour, J. and Chowdhury, G. (2007) Use and Outcome of Online Health Information Services: a study among Scottish population, *Journal of Documentation*, **63** (2), 229–42.

JISC (2009) *Key Findings and Recommendations: final report, November 2009*, National E-Books Observatory Project, JISC, www.jiscebooksproject.org/wp-content/JISC-e-books-observatory-final-report-Nov-09.pdf.

Leedy, P. and Ormrod, J. E. (2009) *Practical Research: planning and design*, 9th edn, Prentice Hall.

Moore, N. (2006) *How to do Research: a practical guide to designing and managing research projects*, 3rd rev. edn, Facet Publishing.

Nicholas, D., Rowlands, I. and Jamali, H. (2010) E-Textbook Use, Information Seeking Behaviour and its Impact: case study business and management, *Journal of Information Science*, **36** (2), 263–80.

Pickard, A. (2007) *Research Methods in Information*, Facet Publishing.

Skykes, J., Dobreva, M., Birrell, D., McCulloch, E., Ruthven, I., Unal, Y. and Feliciati, P. (2010) A New Focus on End Users: eye-tracking analysis for digital libraries, ECDL, 510–13, *Proceedings of the 14th European Conference on Research and Advanced Technology for Digital Libraries*, Springer-Verlag, 2010.

6

Usability data analysis

Introduction

Usability studies, in the words of Rohrer (2008), are 'blessed (or cursed) with a very wide range of research methods, ranging from tried-and-true methods such as lab-based usability studies to those that have been more recently developed, such as desirability studies (to measure aesthetic appeal)'. Indeed, as discussed in Chapter 4, a usability researcher can adopt a variety of approaches and methods for conducting usability research. Irrespective of the study approach – quantitative or qualitative – usability research often generates a large volume and variety of data that needs to be analysed and interpreted appropriately in order to produce useful results and draw appropriate conclusions. If a quantitative approach is adopted, one or more appropriate statistical methods have to be used in order to analyse the data.

Quantitative data can be presented in a variety of ways using tables, charts and so on. Such simple data analysis and presentation techniques provide descriptive statistics as the study findings, but in most statistical studies it is expected that results can be generalized for the entire study population and inferences can be drawn. In doing so, it is also important that the findings are taken with some degrees of confidence, the most common one being a 95% confidence level – the findings can be true for 95% of cases. Depending on its nature and design a usability study may involve a number of data variables that may be independent or dependent on one another, and the data variable may have different characteristics that need to be analysed and interpreted according to appropriate statistical techniques. Consequently, one or more statistical methods need to be used in order to analyse and interpret statistical data properly.

In summary, a usability researcher needs to know at least some of the basic statistical techniques and measures in order to complete a usability study successfully and generate results that can be taken with confidence and generalized appropriately. Again, in addition to employing quantitative analysis techniques, in order to generate statistical data, a usability researcher may also employ some qualitative analysis techniques in order to conduct some in-depth analysis and gather data on specific features and functionalities – for example user preferences and the reasons behind them – of an information product or service. Analysis of such qualitative data also requires specific skills, and some specific tools and techniques need to be employed for the purpose.

This chapter discusses some basic statistical measures commonly used in usability studies and basic approaches to qualitative data analysis techniques. It is by no means comprehensive but can be used as a starting point. With the simple examples provided here, using the most common statistical software packages, such as Microsoft Excel, a researcher will be able to employ some of the most commonly employed statistical techniques to analyse usability data. There are many other software packages available for analysis of statistical data, such as SPSS. Appropriate text and guidebooks for statistical studies should be used for proper description and understanding of various statistical terms, formulae and measurement techniques. Similarly, appropriate texts for analysis of qualitative data and corresponding methods and tools need to be used in order to understand qualitative data analysis techniques.

Data types

A typical usability study generates a variety of different data types on different aspects of an information product or service. Data may be collected on:

- *usage patterns,* such as who uses an information product or service for what purpose, and how frequently
- *levels of satisfaction,* such as how satisfied users are with the overall information service or product and/or specific features and functionalities
- *data traffic,* such as volume and frequency of access to the information product or service, at high and low usage times
- *task completion rates,* such as how many users can successfully complete

specific (assigned or user generated) tasks with the given information product or service

- *success and error rates*, such as how many users can successfully use the specific features and functionalities of the given information product or service, and how often the system generates errors with what message or feedback
- *problems encountered*, such as typical problems that users encounter while using the given information product or service.

A number of variables are used to generate this data, some of which may be independent and others dependent (for the differences see below). Before choosing a statistical measure to analyse the data, a usability researcher should know what type of data is being dealt with and how each type of data has been collected. For example, the usage patterns – number of searches or amount of time spent every day on a specific information product or service – may have been generated for user characteristics like gender, age groups and so on. Similarly data on success and error rates may have been generated for the level of expertise of users or specific tasks, and so on. In order to analyse usability data, a researcher should be familiar with four different types of data: nominal data, ordinal data, interval data and ratio data (Tullis and Albert, 2008).

Independent vs dependent variables

Data variables used in a usability study can be dependent or independent. Independent variables are those that are manipulated in order to generate different data values. For example, in a usability study one might measure the performance of different categories of users that are independent of each other, for example male and female users, expert and novice users, and so on. Independent variables are chosen in accordance with the study objectives and research questions.

Dependent variables are those that are measured for the independent variables. For example, one may try to measure the time taken to accomplish a task, or success or failure rates between two independent variables like expert and novice users, or students and researchers. While independent variables are chosen in accordance with the study objectives and research questions, dependent variables are the data measured and therefore generated by the study. This data is then used to generate findings about the dependent variables and draw conclusions such as the mean task completion time of male compared with female participants, or a correlation between task completion rates and the level of expertise of users.

Nominal vs ordinal data

Nominal data is an unordered group of data that may or may not be represented by nominal values (numbers such as 1, 2, 3) but the nominal values do not have any mathematical or statistical meaning. For example, in a usability study data may be collected for various user categories like male and female students, undergraduate and postgraduate students, novice and expert users, and so on. In order to facilitate coding and using a statistical package, such data groups may be given an ordinal number like 1, 2, 3. In this ordering, each group merely represents a different category of user, but the numbers do not carry their usual meaning: user category 2 is not more (in this context better or worse) than category 1, as their numerical values represent. The researcher has to be careful while coding and analysing nominal data because statistical software packages may use these categories in the context of their numeric values and process the data accordingly.

Ordinal data, as the name suggests, is ordered according to nominal values, but may or may not carry the same meaning of intervals between measurements. For example, in a ranked list of articles, the item on top of the list ranked 1 is not ten times better than the tenth article on the list. The ranked order simply tells us that one is different (more or less) from the other, but the magnitude of the difference cannot be measured with the ordinal value of any two items. In the context of a usability study, if the time taken to accomplish a task is measured across a set of users or a number of searches for the same user it may be possible to arrange the data by the number of seconds (or minutes or even hours) taken to accomplish a task against the percentage of users.

In Table 6.1, four categories of data are presented using nominal values, and in each case the nominal values and their intervals are useful. For example, one may say that 20% people take one minute to complete a task while 30% people take twice as much time – two minutes – to complete the task. Alternatively, one may conclude that the percentage of users who take one minute or two minutes to complete a task is the same as the number taking three or four minutes.

In contrast, Table 6.2 shows ordinal data in the first column, where the

Table 6.1 *Example of ordinal data where intervals between measurements are meaningful*

Time taken to complete a task (minutes)	Percentage of users taking this time
1	20
2	30
3	40
4	10

Table 6.2 *Example of nominal data where intervals between measurements are not meaningful*

Time taken to complete a task (minutes)	Task
1	2
2	3
3	1
4	4

numbers denoting the time taken to accomplish a task is meaningful – data presented in the second row denotes that the time taken to accomplish a task is twice as much as that presented in the first row, or half as much in comparison with the time denoted in the fourth row. The data presented in the second column in Table 6.2 is nominal, where each number just denotes a different task compared with the other, but the arithmetical values of the numbers denoting the tasks do not have any meaning: task 1 and task 2 are simply two different tasks, and one is not twice as difficult or easy as the other.

Thus ordinal data can be used to generate an ordered data set and such a list produces some comparison, but it should be taken with caution because sometimes the figures provide actual comparative data, for example 30% users said the design was very good, 40% users said the design was good and so on, where the two categories of users denote an exact proportion of users. On the other hand, when an interval data is used, for example, in a five-point scale, it is difficult to conclude that a data value at point 2 is twice as good or bad as the data at point 4. These data values simply provide an idea of separation in relation to the data values. For example, 1 is the worst and 5 is the best, or 1 is the slowest and 5 is the fastest in a five-point scale; but not every point is 20% better or worse off than the point next to it – sometimes interval data cannot be measured against one another based on arithmetic values. Use of interval data is very common in usability studies, especially questionnaires, where data is presented using a Likert Scale, which is not an ordinal measure but can be used to rate a particular feature or function of an information product or service.

Descriptive vs inferential statistics

Descriptive statistics present data without any specific inference or conclusions. These statistics can be presented in tables, or statistical software packages can be used to draw graphs and charts for visual representation and comparisons of data. Descriptive statistics do not allow a researcher to draw conclusions about the larger population – whether or to what extent the observed phenomena will hold good for the larger study population – as inferential statistics do. By using inferential statistics, we infer something about a larger population from the smaller sample of study population.

It is impossible to prove that anything is absolutely true using a statistical method. All we do in a statistical analysis is to use a sample and make an informed guess. Therefore, when drawing conclusions from a statistical test we do not aim to prove anything beyond doubt, but say that something is unlikely to happen. If we want to study whether there is a relationship between a particular design and task completion time, or whether there is a relationship between search or task completion time and two categories of users, we must start by hypothesizing that there are no relationships, or making a null hypothesis. The outcome of a statistical analysis is that we either reject, or fail to reject, the null hypothesis. If we can reject the null hypothesis we can say there is a relationship between a particular design and task completion time or that there is a relationship between the user category and task completion time.

Again it is not possible to prove that the conclusion is true in all cases. The degree to which we can be certain that a null hypothesis can be rejected (it is not true) is called the confidence level, which is often denoted by p or alpha and is denoted as 0.01 or 0.05, meaning that there is a 1% or 5% chance that the conclusion may be wrong. Thus if the p value is less than 0.05 we can say with 95% confidence level that the null hypothesis is false and therefore it is rejected and the opposite is true. If the null hypothesis is that there are no relationships between the gender of users and their task completion time, and after conducting the statistical test we get a p value that is less than 0.05, we can say with 95% confidence that the null hypothesis is rejected, or that the study shows there is a relationship between the user's gender and task completion time.

Deciding which statistical technique to use depends on:

- the factors (variables like task completion time, number of errors, and number of search terms used per query) being studied, and the scale and measurements used for the purpose – whether a numerical value is used like time in seconds or minutes, or interval data is generated through a scale like the ease of use or participants' rating of a product feature
- the number of variables and their interrelations or dependencies, for example search or task complexity vs completion time for one or more category of users
- the level of sophistication of variables required to interpret data, for example whether data correlations, dependencies and so on are to be studied (discussed later in this chapter)
- the degree of confidence required for generalization – whether to use 0.01 or 0.05 confidence levels
- the ways in which study participants were selected and allocated for each study group or variable – probabilistic vs non-probabilistic sampling (see Chapter 4)
- the data presentation requirements and inferences to be drawn from the studies, for example whether only descriptive statistics or a combination of descriptive and inferential statistics will be used (for details see the following sections)
- resources – staff, time and software and so on – available for the study.

Table 6.3 overleaf presents some very simple descriptive statistics about the search time for ten users, which can be used as they are or to generate one or more charts for visual comparison.

Using a statistical software package like Excel or SPSS it is possible to generate charts to represent this data visually, and to produce more useful data such as average time taken to search, standard deviation and so on (Table 6.4 overleaf).

Table 6.4 presents a number of statistical terms, which cannot be described in detail in this chapter, but are explained in any textbook on statistics or in any statistical software package (see for example StasSoft, n.d.; Jackson, 1999; and Leedy and Ormrod, 2009). In summary, mean, median and mode are the

Table 6.3 *Search time for ten users undertaking the same task*	
User number	Search time (minutes)
1	29
2	31
3	35
4	42
5	28
6	39
7	32
8	29
9	36
10	34

Table 6.4 *Descriptive statistics on search time for ten users*			
User	Search time (minutes)	Statistical calculation	Search time (seconds)
1	29	Mean	33.5
2	31	Standard error	1.454876856
3	35	Median	33
4	42	Mode	29
5	28	Standard deviation	4.600724581
6	39	Sample variance	21.16666667
7	32	Kurtosis	−0.462290639
8	29	Skewness	0.616130268
9	36	Range	14
10	34	Minimum	28
		Maximum	42
		Sum	335
		Count	10
		Confidence level (95%)	3.291160094

three types of average that denote the central tendency of data. Median is the halfway point of the distribution; in this case half of the search times are below this and the other half are above. Mean denotes the average search time, and mode is the most commonly occurring value, in this case 29. The range is the value denoting the distance between the maximum and minimum data values; in this case the minimum search time is 28 and the maximum search time is 42, hence the range is 14. Variance is a measure that tells us how spread out the data is relative to the mean. Standard deviation, calculated as the square root of variance, shows how much variation or dispersion there is from the mean; a low standard deviation indicates that the data points tend to be very close to the mean; a low standard deviation shows that the mean value is more reliable for the given data set. Kurtosis is a measure of the 'peakedness' of the probability distribution, and skewness is a measure of the asymmetry of the probability distribution of a real-valued random variable. The confidence level mentioned in Table 6.4 is an important concept in usability studies denoting the degree of confidence with which the findings can be taken. Table 6.4 shows that there is a 95% likelihood that the mean search time is 33.5 seconds plus or minus 3.29 seconds.

Parametric vs non-parametric tests

There are two types of tests – parametric and non-parametric – each of which requires a different type of analysis. Many statistical tests are based on the assumption that data is sampled from a normal Gaussian distribution (i.e. the distribution of events in a bell-shaped curve), and called parametric tests. Contrarily, tests that do not make assumptions about the population distribution are called non-parametric tests. Non-parametric tests are chosen when the data does not produce a normal (Gaussian) distribution, for example the time taken to conduct a search or complete a task by a set of study participants will not generate a normal distribution curve. Non-parametric tests are used to analyse nominal and ordinal data (Tullis and Albert, 2008), for example to compare the search times or task completion rates between male and female or expert and novice users. In such cases we do not make any assumptions about the normal distribution of data, and it is very unlikely that the data will be normally distributed. Chi square tests (discussed later in this chapter) are commonly used non-parametric tests in usability studies.

Comparing means: t-tests vs ANOVA tests

Comparing means is a very common statistical test used in usability studies, for example comparing the mean time taken by two different categories of users to accomplish a series of tasks. The choice of the most appropriate statistical test for comparing means depends on the nature and size of the study sample. If one wants to compare the mean time taken to complete a task or a search between two different user groups – say male and female or expert and novice – the measure is for independent samples. For a comparison between two samples a t-test is appropriate; if there are three or more samples, an analysis of variance (ANOVA) test is appropriate.

A t-test is carried out to determine whether the observed data, for example the mean time to accomplish a task by two categories of users, is indeed different. Table 6.5 shows the results of a t-test (generated using Excel) on the average time taken to accomplish a task by two categories of users. The first two columns provide the descriptive data showing the average time taken to complete a task by the two categories of participants – students and staff. We begin with a null hypothesis that there are no relationships between the user category and the average search time. Then a t-test can be conducted using a statistical package like Excel to determine whether there is a statistically significant relationship between the user category and their average task completion time. In Table 6.5, the value p is less than 0.05, so we can reject the null hypothesis and conclude that there is a statistically significant relationship between the user category and average search time.

A paired t-test has to be carried out when means are compared within the same set of participants. For example, one may like to compare the mean task completion time between two different products or designs by the same set of participants. Table 6.6 presents results of a t-test between paired samples generated using Excel.

ANOVA tests are carried out when three or more different samples are compared. Suppose we want to study whether there is a difference in time to complete a task between the three systems. Table 6.7 on page 134 provides the results of a simple ANOVA test, generated using Excel, on task completion time using three different systems. The null hypothesis in ANOVA is that there are no differences – the mean task completion time of the three systems is equal. If the null hypothesis is true, these three systems do not have any significant differences in mean task completion time. The P value in Table 6.7 is more than 0.05, so we fail to reject the null hypothesis. Therefore it can be concluded that there are no statistically significant differences in task completion times between the two systems.

Table 6.5 *T-test: comparing means between two independent samples (average search time for ten tasks for a student and a member of staff)*

Student	Staff		T-test: two-sample assuming equal variances		
15	12			Student	Staff
16	13		Mean	14.1	11.9
12	10		Variance	5.433333333	2.766666667
18	14		Observations	10	10
13	11		Pooled variance	4.1	
11	10		Hypothesized mean difference	0	
14	12		df	18	
13	11		t stat	2.429493574	
12	11		P(T<=t) one-tail	0.012906389	
17	15		t critical one-tail	1.734063592	
			P(T<=t) two-tail	0.025812778	
			t critical two-tail	2.100922037	

Table 6.6 *T-test paired samples: comparing mean time taken to complete a task in two systems*

Task	System1	System2	T-test: paired two sample for means		
1	10	15			
2	16	20		Variable 1	Variable 2
3	12	13	Mean	14.3	15.1
4	17	20	Variance	8.677777778	11.43333333
5	12	12	Observations	10	10
6	15	14	Pearson correlation	0.532090095	
7	14	18	Hypothesized mean difference	0	
8	20	16	df	9	
9	15	13	T stat	−0.820303112	
10	12	10	P(T<=t) one-tail	0.216615596	
			t critical one-tail	1.833112923	
			P(T<=t) two-tail	0.433231192	
			t critical two-tail	2.26215715	

Table 6.7 *A simple ANOVA test*

System 1	System 2	System 3	ANOVA: single factor						
10	15	12							
16	20	18	Summary						
12	13	16	Groups	Count	Sum	Average	Variance		
17	20	12	System 1	10	143	14.3	6.01111111		
12	12	15	System 2	10	155	15.5	10.5		
14	10	17	System 3	10	155	15.5	5.38888889		
15	16	16							
18	17	19							
14	15	16	ANOVA						
15	17	14	Source of variation	SS	df	MS	F	P value	F crit
			Between groups	9.6	6	1.6	0.18670726	0.97757	2.527655
			Within groups	197.1	23	8.5695652			
			Total	206.7	29				

From Table 6.7 it may be noted that the average time taken to accomplish a task in the three systems is fairly similar, but the variance in system 2 is high compared with the two other systems. Can we say that there is no significant difference in the mean task completion time for the three systems?

The F (probability distribution, the ratio of the two variances: 1.56/8.57) value is 0.186 and the critical value we need to achieve 0.5 significance is 2.527. Remember, the null hypothesis was that in all three systems there were no significant differences in the mean task completion times. Since the F statistic is smaller than the critical value, we fail to reject the null hypothesis.

Again the p value can also help find answers our question, whether there is some sort of relationship between the time taken to complete a task and the system being studied. ANOVA assumes by default that there is no relationship. As a general rule, a p value greater than 0.05 means ANOVA's assumption may be right. In this example, the p value is 0.977, which is higher than 0.05, so we can conclude there is no statistically significant relationship between the time taken to accomplish a task and the system being studied.

Correlation analysis

The degree of association between two variables can be determined by a correlation study. Suppose we want to study whether there is a correlation between the number of searches performed and time taken to accomplish a search task by the participants. Table 6.8 shows the results of a correlation study, generated using Excel.

Table 6.8 *Results of a correlation study*					
Participants	Number of search	Time spent on task			
1	5	19		Number of search	Time spent on task
2	6	17	Number of search	1	
3	4	15	Time spent on task	0.684981685	1
4	5	20			
5	3	16			
6	4	15			
7	6	19			
8	7	20			
9	4	14			
10	7	18			

The correlation coefficient r should have a value between −1 to +1; the stronger the correlation, the closer the value of r to −1 or +1; the weaker the relation, the closer the value of r to 0. In this case, the value of r is 0.68, indicating a positive correlation; as the number of searches increases the time spent to accomplish a task also increases.

Chi square tests

The chi square test is a very common non-parametric test used to compare categorical or nominal data, for example to study whether there are any correlations between the search time among male and female participants in a study, or differences in task completion time among users of different age groups. Suppose we want to study if there are any correlations between successful searches and user category. The null hypothesis will be that there are no correlations between the successful searches and user category. Table 6.9 shows the results of such a correlation study generated using Excel. The value of the chi test (calculated automatically by simple software packages such as Excel, SPSS and so on) is 0.036, which is less than 0.05. Therefore we can say there is a statistically significant correlation between user groups and success rates.

Table 6.9 *Results of a chi square test with one variable*

User groups	Actual successful searches	Expected successful searches
UG students	4	8.25
PG students	6	8.25
Researchers	7	8.25
Academics	16	8.25
Total	33	33
Chi square value	0.036075861	

Now suppose we want to conduct the same test with two variables – we are conducting the same search with two different systems and want to measure whether there is any correlation between the success rates and user categories.

The result in Table 6.10 shows that the value of chi square is much less than 0.05 so there is a statistically significant correlation between the success of the user groups and different systems.

Qualitative analysis

Although quantitative approaches are taken in conducting most usability studies in order to generate a variety of statistical data and statistically significant inferences, sometimes qualitative approaches are taken to gather non-numeric data, for example about the general user perceptions and opinions of users on a specific information product or service. Interviews, observations and focus groups generate such qualitative data, which is textual rather than numeric. A variety of data analysis techniques are available for qualitative research and some of them can be used for qualitative usability studies. Several textbooks discuss qualitative data analysis techniques for social science research (for example Denscombe, 2003) and information research (for example Gorman and Clayton, 2005; and Pickard, 2007).

Table 6.10 *Results of a chi square test with two variables*

User group	Success in system A	Success in system B
UG students	4	8
PG students	6	5
Researchers	7	6
Academics	16	14
	Expected success in system A	Expected success in system B
User group		
UG students	8.25	8.25
PG students	8.25	8.25
Researchers	8.25	8.25
Academics	8.25	8.25
Chi square value	0.001040686	

Unlike quantitative analysis, where data on the study participants is collected as an outsider and the analysis process begins only after completing the data collection exercise, qualitative studies require that the researcher becomes part of the group of study subjects, collects data as an insider, and often analyses and makes sense of the data as it is collected. Gorman and Clayton (2005) commented that in order to analyse data a qualitative researcher must move between the roles of scientist and artist. They further suggested (2005, 205) that in a qualitative study the researcher must engage in both convergent thinking, an information processing activity with the goal of 'a single solution or a correct answer', and a divergent thinking, which is 'the creative process of formulating questions, referring to the past experience and cues from the social setting'.

There are four recognized strategies for qualitative data analysis (Pickard, 2007):

- *Phenomenological strategies*: The focus is on discovering the underlying structure of experiences without making any attempt to look for data comparison. This is not very common in usability studies because this method focuses on individual subjects in extreme depth in order to understand and make sense of the phenomenon under study within the specific user context.
- *Ethnographic methods*: The researcher acts as part of a context in which a

phenomenon occurs, the objective being to uncover the social and cultural enactments of the subjects within the given context. This is a useful method in usability studies especially where the aim is to study a specific community and context, and the research aims to find out specific attributes of an information product or service like the design and colour of the interface, use of terminologies and icons with reference to a specific context of culture and so on. It is important that while adopting this method of data collection and analysis the researcher gets immersed in the culture and context of the study subjects and constantly watches, interprets, sifts, sorts and links data as it is gathered.

- *Narrative and discourse analysis*: The aim is to understand how people use and share specific forms of communication, language and understanding. This technique may be useful to compare various information products or services, or different features of a specific information product or service by looking at the language and discourse used and how they are understood and interpreted by the target audience or users. Specific domain and linguistic skills coupled with a good understanding of the context and culture of the user communities – shared meanings and assumptions – are required for this method.
- *Constant comparative analysis*: This is the most commonly adopted approach to qualitative research, involving a strategy of analysis of data and creation of categories driven by raw data as it is collected rather than *a priori* categorization of concepts. This helps the researcher develop an idea of the phenomenon as the study progresses, based on a comparative analysis of the data as it appears.

Coding or deconstructing the data into units with a view to indentifying important concepts, categories and meaning from a huge volume of often unstructured data from interview transcripts, observation notes or focus group notes or video recording is a major activity in qualitative analysis. A variety of coding techniques and software tools like Ethnograph and Nvivo are available for this purpose (Denscombe, 2003; Pickard, 2007). Whatever the technique employed, as Gorman and Clayton (2005, 206) said, 'it follows a nonlinear process of seeing a pattern, returning to the data or the study setting, and exploring or confirming the pattern or an observation with an informant'. Pickard (2007, 242) observed that qualitative analysis 'demands a deep and focused interaction with the raw data, analysing line by line and, in some cases, word by word, and taking nothing at face value'.

Summary

Depending on the objectives, research questions and methods employed, a variety of numeric or textual data is generated in the course of a usability study. Using appropriate methods and tools for analysing the quantitative or qualitative data can help the researcher generate useful findings and conclusions. Some simple quantitative and qualitative analysis techniques are discussed in this chapter. Selection of an appropriate technique for analysis of data depends on a number of factors ranging from the study questions to the nature of the data, expected outcome and, more importantly, availability of resources. Quantitative and qualitative methods both have strengths and weaknesses; statistical methods are used to translate raw data into a meaningful picture for the entire population, and qualitative analyses can provide a deep and context-based understanding of strengths and weaknesses of an information product or service. Ideally a usability study should employ a combination of both techniques in order to achieve the optimum results. Qualitative analyses can be conducted with a fairly small number of study participants, but obtaining reliable statistical results requires more rigorous design and a fairly large sample of study participants (Pearrow, 2007; Rubin and Chisnell, 2008). Coding and analysis of quantitative and qualitative data are resource intensive tasks, requiring research and analytical skills. This should be kept in mind when designing the usability study and choosing data collection and analysis techniques.

References

Denscombe, M. (2003) *The Good Research Guide for Small-Scale Social Research Projects,* 2nd edn, Open University Press.

Gorman, G. E. and Clayton, P. (2005) *Qualitative Research for the Information Professional: a practical handbook,* Facet Publishing.

Jackson, T. (1999) *Introduction to Basic Statistics in Excel,* www.bioss.ac.uk/smart/unix/mbasexc/slides/frames.htm.

Leedy, P. and Ormrod, J. E. (2009) *Practical Research: planning and design,* 9th edn, Prentice Hall.

Pearrow, M. (2007) *Web Usability Handbook,* 2nd edn, Charles River Media.

Pickard, A. J. (2007) *Research Methods in Information,* Facet Publishing.

Rohrer, C. (2008) *When to Use Which User Experience Research Methods,* www.useit.com/alertbox/user-research-methods.html.

Rubin, J. and Chisnell, D. (2008) *Handbook of Usability Testing: how to plan, design and conduct effective tests,* John Wiley.

StatSoft (n.d.) *Electronic Statistics Textbook,* www.statsoft.com/textbook/basic-statistics/.

Tullis, T. and Albert, B. (2008) *Measuring the User Experience: collecting, analyzing and presenting usability metrics,* Morgan-Kaufmann.

7

Web usability

Introduction

The web has brought a major revolution in the way we create, disseminate, access and use information. It has opened new opportunities for creators and users of information products and services because through the web any information product or service can virtually reach every user on the planet. There are challenges, too, because since users are remote, and sometimes unknown, it is often difficult to design an information product or service that would meet the requirements of every potential user. Yet every information product or service developer dreams to use the web to make their products or services available to users, however large or small the user groups are and whether they live next door or thousands of miles apart. All organizations – whether a government organization, an international organization like the United Nations, a city council, a university, a business, a professional organization or a charity – now use the web to make their information products and services available to potential consumers. Some of these information products and services are free, others require consumers to register and pay.

In order to remain competitive on the market, or to constantly improve the quality of their information products or services, organizations need to conduct usability studies. Although it is possible through the web to reach a large number of consumers with an information product or service, a poorly designed website, product or service can easily frustrate and alienate consumers thereby causing a loss of business for the organization. Usability specialists are often employed at every stage of the design of an information product or service, and regular usability studies are conducted once a product or service is on the market in order to detect problems, improve quality and stay competitive. Conducting such usability studies is often challenging, but fortunately a number of guidelines and tools are available for the purpose. This chapter discusses some of the tools and techniques that can be used to conduct usability studies of web-based information services.

What are the challenges?

Although the web has opened up a new vista for reaching the consumers easily and instantly, its very nature has also brought many challenges:

- Potential consumer or users of an information product or service are often far away and it is difficult to model their personalities and behaviour, tasks, information requirements and preferences.
- Different consumer groups and communities have different cultures, expectations, preferences and prejudices, so the one-size-fits-all approach does not work well for web-based information products and services.
- The web is changing constantly and it is becoming a place for fun as well as serious business. Designers therefore need to make sure that it is fun to use an information product or service and at the same time the product helps people do their job, or accomplish specific tasks by gathering and using the required information.
- The web is evolving constantly and user expectations are growing enormously. Many web users have a short attention span, and most do not want to spend a lot of time or effort, yet they want the best out of an online information product or service.
- The regulations governing society are changing and new regulations and standards governing access to and use of the web make the job of designers more challenging because their information products and services need to comply with current legislation.
- Often web users are vulnerable and can be victims of different kinds of unlawful and unpleasant activities; this makes the job of designers more challenging because they need to protect the identity of their customers and ensure their personal information is safe.
- Monitoring the constantly changing behaviour and attitude of web users is technically possible, for example through market scans, transaction log analysis and media reporting. This is very resource intensive, especially for small and medium-sized businesses and information institutions and other organizations – libraries, city councils and so on – whose primary

responsibility is to make information available to their consumers, but which are constantly forced to operate with limited resources.

Pearrow (2007) identified several reasons for a website being unusable:

- Developers focus on the site's features or technical implementation, but do not have any idea about, or do not invest time and effort in understanding, users and their requirements.
- The thinking of technical people in the development team can be completely different from that of end users. Thus the assumptions made by developers often do not match the realities of the lives of users
- Developers tend to use the most state-of-the-art technologies without realizing or testing their real life use and values, and thus often a site becomes technically brilliant but does not meet the end users' requirements.
- People in the design team have very little real life experience of the environment within which an information product or service will be used and therefore their decisions on interface design fail to produce the best results.
- Good websites do not happen by accident nor can they be built only by using the technical expertise of developers; they result from active end user involvement and usability studies at every stage of the product lifecycle.

It is therefore important when designing a good website that the technical expertise of the development team is blended with, and enriched by, the end user experience. A usable website should allow users to perform all the desired functions necessary to meet their information requirements in accomplishing their desired goals with a minimum amount of time and effort.

Which method?

Often a combination of qualitative and quantitative approaches or direct and indirect methods of data collection is adopted in web usability studies. Choosing the most appropriate method for conducting a web usability study is often challenging. Rohrer (2008) suggested that while choosing the study methods, a usability researcher should remember that they differ in three dimensions: attitudinal vs behavioural, qualitative vs quantitative, and in the context of the website or product use.

Attitudinal research usually aims to understand, measure or inform any change of people's stated beliefs; behavioural research aims to understand what people do and why. A combination of direct and indirect approaches can be adopted through surveys, observations, log analyses, eye tracking and so on to obtain the best possible results.

When considering qualitative vs quantitative approaches, it should be remembered that quantitative research generates statistical data, which can be used to generate facts and figures about different product features, usage patterns and so on. Overall, these data sets give an idea of the problems, if any, and show how they are related to various features and functions of an information product or service. Qualitative research provides an insight into exact problems and how to fix them. Thus while quantitative research generates data on usage-specific features and functions, qualitative research offers detailed information about why people like or dislike certain features and functions of a product. Often a combination of qualitative and quantitative methods is used to produce the best results.

Context of use of the information product or service is an important factor to be considered while choosing a usability study method. Although the best option is to collect data from a natural setting with minimum interference, for example through uninterrupted observations, or indirect data collection through video recording or scripts, such approaches also suffer from some problems:

- Use of controlled variation of parameters (for example tasks to be accomplished within a specified period of time, or to be performed by controlled groups like experts and novice users) is not possible.
- Every intended parameter may not be measured because of the researcher's lack of control.
- Task specific data cannot be collected because the researcher is not able to assign specific tasks to the study participants, nor will a number of participants do the same tasks that may be useful for generating comparable statistical data required for the usability study.
- Non-use cannot be captured and data on the non-users cannot be gathered; for example it will not be possible to identify those people who do not use the information product or service under study, so it will not be possible to find out why people do not use it.

Sometimes hybrid methods can be useful to generate data on what people do and don't use, and then find out why they made certain choices.

User-centred design and accessibility issues

The principle of user-centred design is based on the mantra 'know thy user' (Pearrow, 2007). Thus user-centred design puts users ahead of anything else, and the entire design process is governed, at least in principle, by user needs. International standards like ISO 9241-210:2010 prescribe specific guidelines for user-centred design. Pearrow (2007) suggested that user-centred design has five key stages:

- Plan the human centred process.
- Specify the context of use.
- Specify user and organizational requirements.
- Produce design solutions.
- Evaluate designs against user requirements.

As may be noted, gathering information about users and context begins way before the actual design begins, and once a website has been designed it is subjected to evaluation against specified user requirements. Gathering information about users begins with finding out basic information: who they are; what their level of education and ICT and internet literacy is; where they live; what their age, gender, income level, social and personal behaviour is; what they do; what information they need and from where; and so on. Subsequently more specific information is gathered about users' habits, preferences, minimum functional requirements of the website concerned, specific constraints and so on. Information about users' daily activities is gathered and analysed for specific information requirements, then more information is obtained on how information requirements are currently being met, what existing websites or systems users use, and so on. Much of this information is personal and there may be restrictions over how it is gathered and used, often covered by ethical guidelines on usability research. Usability researchers should:

- brief study participants about the nature of the study, and the expected time and effort required from them while taking part
- ensure that study participants are not disadvantaged in any way because of their participation in the study

- not force participants to take part in the study; participation should be voluntary
- not expect participants to answer all the questions or attend all the sessions, and they should be free to leave at any point in time
- not compel participants to perform any task that they do not wish to perform or are uncomfortable with
- never fool or deceive participants
- use information gathered through the study anonymously
- use information gathered entirely for the stated study and not reveal it to anyone
- tell participants about the usability study or research and its objectives, especially those related to the role they are expected to play in the study
- allow participants to ask questions and to clarify any aspect of the questions they are asked or tasks they are required to perform.

Web usability and accessibility

Usability and accessibility are closely related concepts, which complement each other. In order to make a website usable one should ensure that the site is accessible to all kinds of people and take appropriate measures to ensure that those with certain disabilities are not disadvantaged. The 1999 Web Content Accessibility Guidelines of the World Wide Web Consortium (W3C) remind us that a web content developer should remember that some users may:

- not be able to see, hear or move, or may be unable to process some types of information easily or at all
- have difficulty reading or comprehending text
- not have or be able to use a keyboard or mouse
- have a text-only screen, a small screen, or a slow internet connection
- not speak or understand fluently the language in which the document is written
- be in a situation where their eyes, ears or hands are busy or interfered with (for example driving to work or working in a loud environment)
- have an early version of a browser, a different browser entirely, a voice browser or a different operating system.

A usable website should accommodate all types of user, with or without disabilities. Web Content Accessibility Guidelines (WCAG) 2.0 (W3C, 2008) provide a wide range of recommendations for making web content more accessible:

- *Principles*: Four principles provide the foundation for web accessibility.
- *Guidelines*: There are 12 guidelines that web content developers should follow in order to make content more accessible to users with different disabilities.
- *Success criteria*: For each guideline there is a set of testable success criteria that should be used where requirements and conformance testing are necessary, such as design specification, purchasing, regulation and contractual agreements.
- *Sufficient and advisory techniques*: For each of the guidelines and success criteria a wide variety of techniques may be followed to achieve individual success criteria and address the guidelines.

WCAG 2.0 Principles and Guidelines are listed in Table 7.1 overleaf. A variety of government standards and guidelines have also appeared over the years in order to guide people in developing usable and accessible websites. For example, in the USA, Usability.gov (www.usability.gov/) is the primary government source providing guidance and tools on usability and user-centered design of websites. Similar policies and guidelines are also available from other governments; see for example http://australia.gov.au/about/accessibility. The British Standards Institution (BSI) has recently published BS 8878:2010, the first UK web accessibility standard requiring web owners to make their websites accessible for disabled and older users. However, these are relatively recent efforts and a closer look at most currently available websites demonstrates that they are a long way from complying with prescribed accessibility guidelines. Nevertheless, many organizations are now persuading governments and other agencies to meet the web accessibility guidelines.

Usability metrics and heuristic evaluation

As discussed earlier in the book, Nielsen (2001) identified four common metrics for measuring the usability of a website, which Pearrow (2007) reproduced as:

Table 7.1 *WCAG 2.0 principles and guidelines (W3C, 2008)*

WCAG 2.0 principles	WCAG 2.0 guidelines
Principle 1 Be perceivable: information and user interface components must be presentable to users in ways they can perceive	Guideline 1.1 Give text alternatives: provide text alternatives for any non-text content so it can be changed into other forms people need, such as large print, braille, speech, symbols or simpler language
	Guideline 1.2 Allow for time-based media: provide alternatives for time-based media
	Guideline 1.3 Be adaptable: create content that can be presented in different ways (for example in a simpler layout) without losing information or structure
	Guideline 1.4 Be distinguishable: make it easier for users to see and hear content including separating foreground from background
Principle 2 Be operable: user interface components and navigation must be operable	Guideline 2.1 Be keyboard accessible: make all functionality available from a keyboard
	Guideline 2.2 Allow enough time: provide users enough time to read and use content
	Guideline 2.3 Avoid seizures: do not design content in a way that is known to cause seizures
	Guideline 2.4 Be navigable: provide ways to help users navigate, find content and determine where they are
Principle 3 Be understandable: information and the operation of the user interface must be understandable	Guideline 3.1 Be readable: make text content readable and understandable
	Guideline 3.2 Be predictable: make web pages appear and operate in predictable ways
	Guideline 3.3 Give input assistance: help users avoid and correct mistakes
Principle 4 Be robust: content must be robust enough that it can be interpreted reliably by a wide variety of user agents, including assistive technologies	Guideline 4.1 Be compatible: maximize compatibility with current and future user agents, including assistive technologies

- *success rate*: defined by a user accomplishing a usability task within the specified constraints such as completion time or goal state
- *total time*: defined as the time required to complete a task measured in seconds

- *error rate*: measuring the percentage of times a user fails to accomplish a specified task
- *users' subjective satisfaction*: scored in a scale to measure how users feel about their performance and the overall site.

Heuristic or expert evaluation is the most commonly used approach to conduct usability study of websites. A heuristic evaluation is conducted by specialists based on some agreed principles or heuristics. Nielsen (2005) proposed a ten-step heuristic evaluation technique, which is widely used for conducting usability studies of websites. These guidelines largely focus on the interface design and some functionalities of the product, and are somewhat similar to the interface guidelines prescribed a long time ago by the human–computer interface guru Shneiderman (Shneiderman and Plaisant, 2010):

- *Visibility of system status*: The site should tell users what is going on and provide feedback within a reasonable time.
- *Match between system and the real world*: The site should use users' language – words, phrases and concepts – and follow real-world conventions in organizing and using information, symbols and so on.
- *User control and freedom*: Users should be able to exit the site whenever they want and the exit route should be clearly signposted.
- *Consistency and standards*: The site should use terms, phrases, symbols and conventions consistently so they mean the same thing wherever they appear on a site.
- *Error prevention*: Error-prone conditions should be eliminated altogether or users should be given a message before they commit to the action that may lead to an error.
- *Recognition rather than recall*: Users should not have to remember specific actions or dialogues. Users' memory load should be minimized by making objects, actions and options visible or easily retrievable whenever possible.
- *Flexibility and efficiency of use*: A site should cater to both inexperienced and experienced users; frequent users should be able to tailor actions.
- *Aesthetic and minimalist design*: Irrelevant information should be avoided as far as practicable and a minimalist approach should be taken to providing information to users about the site and/or specific activities.
- *Help users recognize, diagnose and recover from errors*: Error messages should be expressed in plain language by precisely indicating the problem, and constructively suggesting a solution.

- *Help and documentation*: Even though it is better if the system can be used without documentation, it may be necessary to provide help and documentation. Any help information should be user task related, easy to search and list specific steps to be carried out.

These heuristic evaluation guidelines enable experts to assess the general usability features of any website, but other usability measures may be needed to measure the usability of specific features and functionalities of online information products or services. These are discussed in the next chapter.

Summary

Web technology, user needs and user expectations from web-based information products and services, and the guidelines and standards governing the creation of websites, have changed over the years. Consequently the heuristic evaluation guidelines listed above need to be modified and/or extended to meet the requirements of modern day websites. W3C accessibility guidelines, international and national standards for user-centred design of websites have given rise to new usability parameters for websites.

Some researchers (for example, Spiliotopoulos et al., 2010) propose that usability methods for the web can be classified into four groups: inquiry, prototyping, inspection and testing methods. Inquiry methods investigate the usability attributes of a system as determined by users through personas, card sorting, questionnaires, interviews, focus groups, observations and so on. Prototyping methods aim to model the website based on the business objectives of the organization producing the information product or service and identified user requirements. Usability prototyping methods include paper prototyping, storyboards, video prototyping, rapid prototyping and parallel design (for details of these methods see Spiliotopoulos et al., 2010). Inspection methods include evaluation of websites by one or more experts using heuristic evaluation, cognitive reviews and walk-throughs. Testing methods involve using actual users in the evaluation of a website using a variety of usability techniques discussed earlier in this chapter and in Chapter 4.

Coupled with increasing competitiveness and changing business objectives, companies and businesses are facing some challenges from emerging social networking technologies that can act as both positive or negative marketing tools for web-based information products and services because good or bad news (about an information product or service) can be spread throughout the world within a matter of minutes through social networks. Yet, businesses – companies, universities, businesses and charities – increasingly use social networking tools like Facebook and YouTube to attract users. Because of the universal nature of the web, researchers and developers are now challenged by what is called the universal usability of websites and web-based information products and services. Factors that affect, or have a significant influence on, universal usability include (Shneiderman, and Plaisant, 2010):

- variations in physical ability and workplace of users
- diverse cognitive and perceptual abilities of users
- personality differences of users
- the cultural and international diversity of users
- disabilities and special needs of users
- special facilities needed by senior adult users
- special facilities needed by child users
- diverse and emerging hardware and software technologies.

Designers of web-based information products and services are often confronted with the challenges of meeting specific user needs rather than achieving universal usability.

References

BS 8878:2010 *Web Accessibility: code of practice*, British Standards Institution.

ISO 9241-210:2010 *Ergonomics of Human-System Interaction – Part 210: human-centred design for interactive systems*, International Organization for Standardization.

Nielsen, J. (2001) *Usability Metrics*, www.useit.com/alertbox/20010121.html.

Nielsen, J. (2005) *Ten Usability Heuristics*, www.useit.com/papers/heuristic/heuristic_list.html.

Pearrow, M. (2007) *Web Usability Handbook*, 2nd edn, Charles River Media.

Rohrer, C. (2008) *When to Use Which User Experience Research Methods*, www.useit.com/alertbox/user-research-methods.html.

Shneiderman, B. and Plaisant, C. (2010) *Designing the User Interface: strategies for effective human-computer interaction*, 5th edn, Addison-Wesley.

Spiliotopoulos, T., Papadopoulou, P., Martakos, D. and Kouroupetroglou, G. (eds)

(2010) *Integrating Usability Engineering for Designing the Web Experience: methodologies and principles,*. Information Science Reference.

W3C (1999) *Web Content Accessibility Guidelines 1.0,* www.w3.org/TR/WAI-WEBCONTENT/wai-pageauth.pdf.

W3C (2008) *Web Content Accessibility Guidelines (WCAG) 2.0: W3C Recommendation 11 December,* www.w3.org/TR/WCAG20/.

8

The usability of digital libraries

Introduction

Usability studies of digital libraries primarily aim to find out how easily users can interact with the interface of the digital library, find useful information and use retrieved information to accomplish specific tasks, and what their general impressions about the various features and functionalities of the library are. Some usability studies also aim to gather information about the non-users with a view to finding out why potential users don't use the digital library, and what can be done to make it usable for them.

Chowdhury, Landoni and Gibb (2006) suggested that usability of a digital library depends on a number of factors, such as the effectiveness and efficiency of the information access system, the ease of use and friendliness of the user interface, users' needs, usage patterns and so on. Sumner (2005) emphasized that understanding the needs and type of work of users, and innovative user interfaces and interaction mechanisms can influence better use of digital library resources, collections and services. Park (2000) observed that the heterogeneity and distribution of information resources is also an important usability factor. Bishop et al. (2000) pointed out that a digital library is a space where users engage with the information infrastructure, so user problems, user attitudes, specific use situations and work practices are important points for usability studies.

There have been a number of usability and evaluation studies of digital libraries over the past two decades, which have used a variety of usability study techniques and methods of data collections and analysis. Several models for usability and evaluation of digital libraries have also been proposed by researchers. This chapter discusses various issues related to the usability of digital libraries and discusses the factors that researchers have identified as important for usability studies of digital libraries. Finally it discusses some usability study models, with particular reference to MEDLIS, a usability study model developed by one of the authors of this book in the course of a research project.

Approaches to digital library usability studies

Evaluation of user interfaces has been particularly popular in usability studies of digital libraries. Several researchers (Marchionini and Komlodi, 1998; Norlin, 2000; Choudhury, Hobbs and Lorie, 2002) have noted that most digital library usability studies have emphasized the human–computer interaction (HCI) factors such as interfaces, especially in assessing their effectiveness, efficiency and/or user satisfaction. Research on the usability of digital libraries have broadly used two main approaches:

- empirical techniques, which involve testing systems with users
- analytical techniques, which involve experts assessing systems and heuristic evaluation, using established theories and methods.

Sandusky (2002) described a framework for evaluating the usability of different types of digital libraries; audience, institution, access, content, services, design and development are the attributes included in the framework. Kim (2002) reported on an empirical model for usability called the Digital Library Information Seeking Process (DLISP), which establishes the events that occur in chronological order when users interact with a digital library and users' perceived difficulties while interacting with the system. The model can be particularly useful for the evaluation and redesign of a digital library. Blandford et al. (2004) reported on a set of four different techniques: heuristic evaluation, cognitive walk-through, claims analysis and concept-based evaluation. They suggested that scenarios can be useful for understanding new situations in digital libraries.

Dillon (2005) pointed out that the human factors of interface design for information usage were best thought of as physical, perceptual and socio-cognitive levels of users. He proposed a qualitative framework for a usability study of digital libraries that focuses on four elements:

- *task*: what users want to do
- *information model*: what structures of the digital library aid use of information

- *manipulation of materials*: how users access the components of the document
- *ergonomics of visual displays*: how visual displays affect human perception of information.

Usability factors in digital libraries

Blandford and Buchanan (2003) listed the following criteria for assessing the usability of digital libraries:

- *achieving goals*: how effectively and efficiently users can achieve their goals with a digital library system
- *learnability*: how easily users learn to use the digital library
- *help and error recovery*: how well the digital library helps users avoid making errors, or recover from errors
- *user experience*: how much users enjoy working with the digital library
- *context*: how well the system fits within the context in which it is used.

Arguing that user requirements change from one search session to another, or even within a given search session, Bollen and Luce (2002) pointed out that usability factors such as user preferences and satisfaction tend to be highly transient and specific; for example, the user search focus can shift from one subject domain to another between, or even within, retrieval sessions. Therefore, they recommend that research on these issues needs to focus on more stable characteristics of a given user community, such as 'the community's perspective on general document impact and the relationships between documents in a collection'.

Checklist of usability features

Chowdhury (2004) provided a checklist of usability features for digital libraries from the perspectives of user interface and information retrieval features.

Interface features

Interface features include:

- types of interface (for example simple vs expert search interfaces)
- language(s) of the interface
- navigation options, shortcuts and system information
- screen features such as use of colour, typography, layout and graphics
- personalization of the interface, for example choice of interface language and/or retrieval level, number of records on one page and sort options.

Search process: database or resource selection

Search process features include:

- options for selection
- cross-database search facilities.

Query formulation facilities

Query formulation facilities include:

- formulation and modification of queries
- building search sets
- saving searches.

Search options

Search options include:

- specific search options for text, multimedia, specific collection and so on
- multiple access points or search fields.

Search operators

Search operators include:

- use of search operators
- natural language queries.

Results manipulation

Results manipulation includes:

- format(s) for display of records
- the number of records that can be displayed
- navigation in the list of records
- marking of the records
- sort options
- printing, exporting and e-mailing of records.

Help features

Help features include:

- appropriateness and usefulness
- context-sensitive help
- consistency of terminology, design and layout
- linguistic correctness.

Other factors

The patterns of interactions between a user and a system can be studied through usability research. One may look for answers to such questions as what users are looking for, how easily they can find the required information, what inhibits them from using a digital library, and so on. Stelmaszewska and Blandford (2002) identified seven stages of information interaction in digital libraries: initiation, selection, exploration, query formulation, result examination, document collection and results presentation. They conclude that patterns identified in this study hold crucial knowledge about users' behaviour that can provide a basis for understanding what users do when looking for specific information.

Sometimes users find that the interface is a common barrier to accessing a digital library. User interfaces should be designed to be simple to understand, easy to use and interactive. Peng, Ramaiah and Foo (2004) conducted a usability study of the interface of the hybrid library of Nanyang Technological University in Singapore using Nielsen and Levy's (1994) user interface heuristics. The general conclusion of the study was that contrary to the popular belief, an attractive and graphical user interface is not necessarily simple and easy to use.

Cultural issues are often very important considerations and play a vital role in the use and impact of a user interface. Liew (2005) discussed the usability and user interface features of a digital library of Maori cultural heritage. Emphasizing the importance of cultural issues on the usability of information services, Duncker, Theng and Mohd-Nasir (2000) commented that misinterpretation of the importance of colours, forms, symbols, metaphors and language for users from different cultural backgrounds can significantly affect the usability and friendliness of digital libraries. Some digital library evaluation studies have focused on usability from the perspectives of the organization of, and access to, information resources. These studies are often classed as personalized digital libraries. For example, Meyyappan, Chowdhury and Foo (2001) and Meyyappan, Foo and Chowdhury (2004) have reported on the usability of a prototype task-based digital library where they have studied the task-based information organization and access system.

Many researchers have conducted usability studies to find out how digital libraries are used by target users to accomplish their tasks or meet their information needs. Probably one of the earliest and most widely known impact studies was conducted by Borgman and her colleagues (Borgman, 2002, 2004; Borgman et al., 2000, 2004, 2005; Borgman and Rassmussen, 2005) in the context of the Alexandria Digital Library. Borgman et al. (2000) provided an observation of undergraduate students' use of ADEPT in the classroom. Leazer, Gilliland-Swetland and Borgman (2000) and Leazer et al. (2000) investigated the impact of ADEPT on teaching and learning in undergraduate classes. Borgman et al. (2004, 2005) also discussed how academics used the geographical information for preparing their lecture notes compared with their research activities. Champeny et al. (2004) discussed the development of a digital learning environment and its implementation in undergraduate geography courses. They also reported some interesting findings; for example an instructor found her usability of the library increased from one term to another; classroom presentations seemed to be useful for understanding concepts; and web access to presentations was useful for study and review.

Digital library usability study models and techniques

The Perseus Digital Library (PDL) was developed to assess the impact on users in the field of humanities (Marchionini, 2000). Data was collected through multiple methods such as observations (baseline, structured, participant), think aloud, transaction log analysis, interviews, document analysis and learning analysis. The National Science Digital Library (NSDL) evaluation studies used a variety of methods, such as log analysis, survey instruments, collection assessment techniques and interviews, in order to examine library usage, collection growth and library governance processes (Jones and Sumner, 2002).

Pan et al. (2004) evaluated the Kinetic Models for Design Digital Library (KMODDL), based on the context, interaction, attitude and outcomes (CIAO!) framework. The aim of this evaluation was to identify and assess the integration of KMODDL resources into middle school and university undergraduate classes to facilitate better learning and understanding. Maly et al. (n.d.) proposed two alternative frameworks for digital library evaluation. In the first approach, the evaluator identifies the necessary, desirable and undesirable characteristics of digital libraries for undergraduate science education, and the project is then assessed against these characteristics. In the second approach the evaluator first proposes some hypotheses for evaluating the impact, identifies the characteristics for these hypotheses, and then identifies and implements measures to validate the hypotheses.

Madle et al. (2003) proposed a methodology for evaluating the impact of the National Electronic Library for Communicable Disease (NeLCD) on users' knowledge, attitudes and behaviour. This methodology combines transaction log analysis and a questionnaire of pre- and post-use of the digital library, which helps assess the impact of the library on users and their work and evaluate the usability of a digital library. In this context, Nicholas, Huntington and Williams (2003) noted that while evaluating users' knowledge, attitude and behaviour, a small number of users always gives a clearer picture about the behaviour of individual users. Sumner and Marlino (2004) proposed three approaches – using cognitive tools, component repositories and knowledge networks – with specific examples drawn from the Digital Library for Earth System Education (DLESE) and the NSDL for educational digital libraries. They concluded that the three approaches can help to deconstruct the digital library metaphor to generate better understandings about the impact of a library on educational practice. They also claimed that these three models can reflect the complex interactions between humans, technology and context in educational digital libraries.

Usability studies conducted by members of the Digital Library Federation

A variety of research methods and techniques have been used in the course of various usability and evaluation studies of digital libraries conducted within the Digital Library Federation (DLF) (www.clir.org/pubs/reports/pub105/section4.html), including think aloud, transaction log and systems analysis, heuristic evaluation, card sorting and survey research. A typical example of the usability study conducted by a DLF member involves the following steps (Covey, 2002):

- Conducted a heuristic evaluation of the existing library Web site
- Looked at other Web sites to find sites its members liked
- Created a profile of different user types (for example, new or novice users, disabled users)
- Created a list of what the redesigned Web site had to do, organized by priority
- Created a content list of the current Web site that revealed content of interest only to librarians (for example, a list of library organizations)
- Created a content list for the redesigned Web site that eliminated any content in the existing site that did not fit the user profiles
- Conducted a card sorting study to help group items on the content list
- Conducted a Web-based survey to help determine the vocabulary for group and item (link) labels. (The survey did not work very well because the groups and items the participants were to label were difficult to describe.)
- Implemented a prototype of the new library Web site home page and secondary pages
- Conducted think-aloud protocols with the prototype Web pages. (The library recruited and screened participants to get eight subjects. The subjects signed consent forms, then did the protocol tasks. Different task scripts were provided for undergraduate students, graduate students, and faculty. The protocols were audiotaped and capture software was used to log participant keystrokes. The facilitator also took notes during the protocols. The results of the protocol study revealed that many of the problems users encountered were not user interface problems, but bibliographic instruction problems.)
- Conducted a survey questionnaire to capture additional information about the participants' experience and perception of the new Web site.

Usability studies of Europeana Digital Library

Using a combination of focus group methods and eye tracking technologies, a group of researchers recently conducted usability studies of one of the world's largest live digital libraries, called the Europeana, a digital library for researchers, professionals and the public, giving a single access point to Europe's cultural heritage linking up to digitized content from memory institutions across Europe. The usability study focused on a number of areas, including (Dobreva and Chowdhury, 2010):

- ease of use and intuitiveness of Europeana especially in the case of users who visit the website for the first time
- identification of 'future' user needs as the young generation grows up
- styles of use of the prototype for knowledge discovery among young users
- expectations, including how users see trustworthiness
- similarities and differences in the groups from different countries.

Usability data was gathered from selected participant groups in four countries – Bulgaria, Italy, the Netherlands and the UK – and media labs held in the UK. Data collection included completed questionnaires, recordings of discussion sessions, the populated presentations, queries saved in My Europeana by each participant and eye tracking data (Dobreva and Chowdhury, 2010). User tasks were set using eight different scenarios:

- finding texts on a predefined topic
- finding images on a predefined topic
- finding audio and video materials on a predefined topic
- finding materials presenting the same object in different times
- finding materials on a very specific subject (such as a landmark, an event or a person)
- finding materials on a topic of the participant's choice within the context of the general theme
- finding materials on a specific time period or event which happened on a specific date
- identifying providers of digital objects who contributed the highest number of objects on a particular topic, analysing what was found to be most useful about Europeana and suggesting areas in which material may be lacking.

Usability findings were then discussed, based on three categories of users' impressions:

- *first impressions*: what users expect from Europeana
- *deeper impressions*: what users experience
- *lasting impressions*: whether or not users are willing to use Europeana in future and what improvements are required for future use.

Data collected through this study was visualized as heat maps and gaze plots to study the participants' eye movements as they interacted with the European interface (Skykes et al., 2010). The researchers noted that eye tracking data used in conjunction with the other data gathered through other usability methods can provide reliable data and insights into users' information behaviour as well as the actual usage patterns, preferences and so on.

MEDLIS: a digital library usability model

Chowdhury, McMenemy and Poulter (2008) developed and tested a generic model called MEDLIS for usability and evaluation of digital libraries. They recommended that a digital library usability study should begin with some broad questions, and it is important to find out who should best provide the answers to the questions. For example, information related to the origin and objectives of the digital library service, the management and business model and so on, can be obtained from the management and the service website. Although some of this information can also be obtained by studying various documents – minutes of meetings, memos, design documents and so on – access to some information is usually restricted and can be obtained only through agreement with the management. Similarly, some information, such as the reasons for using the service, ease of use of the service and user satisfaction rates can only be obtained from users.

Some digital libraries and information services are provided through libraries where library and information science professionals play several important roles, ranging from marketing and promotion to providing user support, or even acting as intermediaries by conducting searches on behalf of users. Under such circumstances, significant amounts of valuable inform-ation can be obtained from these intermediaries. Nevertheless, information collected from each stage of the evaluation can be compared with, substantiated by, or used in combination with the information collected from other phases of the evaluation study. The last column of the MEDLIS framework (Figure 8.1, overleaf) lists the possible methods that can be used to collect the necessary information. The list is obviously not exhaustive, and one may apply one or more appropriate research methods to collect information depending on the situation – nature of the digital library, users, usability study objectives and so on.

As the MEDLIS framework (Figure 8.1) shows, any digital library usability study should begin by addressing two basic questions: what is the service all about, and who provides it? To find answers to these questions easily and appropriately one should study the website of the digital library service, and work with the management team responsible for the design and daily management of the service. There are two sets of tasks to be managed in a digital library service. Although in some cases they may both be the responsibility of the same management team or organization, it is appropriate to distinguish between the activities involved: tasks related to the design, development, maintenance, delivery and management of the overall digital library service; and those related to creating the service (from a strategic perspective) and providing necessary resources. Information on a number of pertinent issues, such as the objectives and targeting of the service, management policies, economic models and design policies, can be obtained by conducting surveys of the management team, analysing pertinent documents, and critically studying the usage statistics.

The MEDLIS framework shows links between various usability study questions, possible sources of required information, possible methods for collecting data, and factors or points to be studied in each case. Answers to some questions can be obtained from more than one source and the necessary information may be obtained using different methods. For example, as shown in Figure 8.1 overleaf, the effectiveness of the digital library can be assessed by consulting the end users of the service, but further information may be obtained from transaction log analysis, and by surveying intermediaries (information professionals who deliver the service at the users' end). These intermediaries make comments on usage patterns and user satisfaction based on their day-to-day experience of serving users, and the uniqueness and effectiveness of the given service in comparison with other services that provide access to similar types of information.

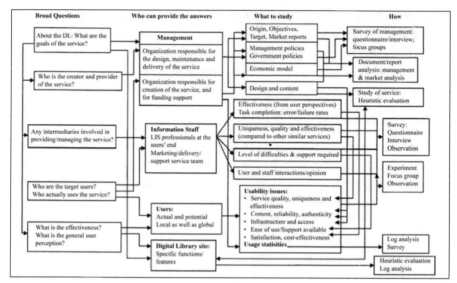

Figure 8.1   *MEDLIS: a generic framework for usability and evaluation of digital libraries*

Summary

The usability studies discussed in this chapter have reported different kinds of usability features and characteristics of specific digital libraries and information resources. They illustrate that in addition to the technical issues of digital library design architecture, information retrieval tools and user interfaces, there are a number of usability issues related to digital libraries, such as:

- globalization and localization
- specific language materials and multilingual information
- access and management
- culture, traditions and cross-cultural and multicultural factors
- content – homogeneous and heterogeneous information resources, mono-multimedia resources, local and distributed information resources and so on
- human information behaviour issues, especially when users are remote and distributed.

This chapter shows that researchers adopt a variety of methods and techniques to gather data on the usability of digital libraries. 'Know thy user' is the mantra of any usability study, and consequently all digital library usability studies discussed in this chapter have focused on end users. In designing the MEDLIS model, Chowdhury, McMenemy and Poulter (2008) suggested that usability studies should consider both end users and intermediaries – library and information professionals – since the latter group are in direct touch with users and consequently can provide much valuable information.

References

Bishop, A. P., Peterson, L. J., Neumann, S. L., Star, M. C., Ignacio, E. and Sandusky, R. J. (2000) Digital Libraries: situating use in changing information infrastructure, *Journal of the American Society for Information Science*, **51** (4), 394–13.

Blandford, A. and Buchanan, G. (2003) Usability of Digital Libraries: a source of creative tensions with technical developments, *TCDL Bulletin*, www.ieee-tcdl.org/Bulletin/current/blandford/blandford.html.

Blandford, A., Keith, S., Connell, I. and Edwards, H. (2004) Analytical Usability Evaluation for Digital Libraries: a case study. In *Proceedings of the 2004 Joint ACM/IEEE Conference on Digital Libraries*, http://portal.acm.org.

Bollen, J. and Luce, R. (2002) Evaluation of Digital Library Impact and User Communities by Analysis of Usage Patterns, *D-Lib Magazine*, **8** (6), www.dlib.org/dlib/june02/bollen/06bollen.html.

Borgman, C. and Rasmussen, E. (2005) Usability of Digital Libraries in a Multicultural Environment. In Theng, Y.-L. and Foo, S. (eds), *Design and Usability of Digital Libraries: case studies in the Asia-Pacific*, Information Science Publishing, 270–84.

Borgman, C. L. (2002) Evaluation of Digital Libraries: testbeds, measurements, and metrics. Paper given at *Fourth DELOS Workshop. Computer and Automation Research Institute (MTA SZTAKI), Hungarian Academy of Sciences, Budapest, Hungary, 6–7 June 2002*, final report to the National Science Foundation, www.sztaki.hu/conferences/deval/presentations/FINAL%20REPORT%20TO%20NSF%20CISE_10_2.doc.

Borgman, C. L. (2004) Evaluating the Uses of Digital Libraries. Paper given at *DELOS Workshop on Evaluation of Digital Libraries, Padova, Italy*, www.delos.info/eventlist/wp7_ws_2004/Borgman.pdf.

Borgman, C. L., Gilliland-Swetland, A. J., Leazer, G. L., Mayer, R., Gwynn, D., Gazan, R. and Mautone, P. (2000) Evaluating Digital Libraries for Teaching and Learning in Undergraduate Education: a case study of the Alexandria Digital

Earth Prototype (ADEPT), *Library Trends*, special issue, **49** (2), 228–50.

Borgman, C. L., Leazer, G. H., Gilliland-Swetland, A., Millwood, K., Champeny, L., Finley, J. and Smart, L .J. (2004) How Geography Professors Select Materials for Classroom Lectures: implications for the design of digital libraries. In *Proceedings of the 4th ACM/IEEE-CS Joint Conference on Digital Libraries, Tucson, Arizona*, 179–85.

Borgman, C. L., Smart, L. J., Millwood, K. A., Finley, J. R., Champeny, L., Gilliland, A. J. and Leazer, G. H. (2005) Comparing Faculty Information Seeking in Teaching and Research: implications for the design of digital libraries, *Journal of the American Society for Information Science*, **56** (6), 636–57.

Champeny, L., Borgman, C. L., Leazer, G. H., Gilliland-Swetland, A. J., Millwood, K. A., D'Avolio, L., Finley, J. R., Smart, L. J., Mautone, P. D., Mayer, R. E., Johnson, R. A., Chen, H., Christel, M. and Lim, E.-P. (2004) Developing a Digital Learning Environment: an evaluation of design and implementation processes. In *Proceedings of the 2004 Joint ACM/IEEE Conference on Digital Libraries, Tucson, Arizona, ACM, New York*, 37–46.

Choudhury, S., Hobbs, B. and Lorie, M. (2002) A Framework for Evaluating Digital Library Services, *D-Lib Magazine*, **8** (7/8), www.dlib.org/dlib/july02/choudhury/07choudhury.html.

Chowdhury, G., McMenemy, D. and Poulter, A. (2008) MEDLIS: Model for Evaluation of Digital Libraries and Information Services, *World Digital Libraries*, **1** (1), 35–46

Chowdhury, G. G. (2004) Access and Usability Issues of Scholarly Electronic Publications. In Gorman, G. E. and Rowland, F. (eds), *Scholarly Publishing in an Electronic Era: International Yearbook of Library and Information Management*, 2004–2005, Facet Publishing, 77–98.

Chowdhury, S., Landoni, M. and Gibb, F. (2006) Usability and Impact of Digital Libraries: a review, *Online Information Review*, **30** (6), 656–80.

Covey, D. T. (2002) Usage and Usability Assessment: library practices and concerns, Digital Library Federation, Council on Library and Information, www.diglib.org/pubs/dlf096/dlf096.pdf.

Dillon, A. (2005) Evaluating on Time: a framework for the expert evaluation of digital library interface usability, www.ischool.utexas.edu/adillon/publications/evaluating.html.

Dobreva, M. and Chowdhury, S. (2010) A User-Centric Evaluation of the Europeana Digital Library. In Chowdhury, G., Khoo, C. and Hunter, J. (eds), The Role of Digital Libraries in a Time of Global Change, *[Proceedings of the] 12th International Conference on Asia-Pacific Digital Libraries, ICADL 2010, Gold Coast, Australia, June 21–25*, 148–57.

Duncker, E., Theng, Y. L. and Mohd-Nasir, N. (2000) Cultural Usability in Digital Libraries, *Bulletin of the American Society for Information Science*, **26** (4), 21–22, www.asis.org/Bulletin/May-00/duncker__et_al.html.

Jones, C. and Sumner, T. (2002) Evaluation of the National Science Digital Library, www.uclic.ucl.ac.uk/annb/docs/JonesSumner5.pdf.

Kim, K. (2002) A Model-Based Approach to Usability Evaluation for Digital Libraries. In Blandford, A. and Buchanan, G. (eds), *JCDL '02 Workshop on Usability of Digital Libraries*, www.uclic.ucl.ac.uk/annb/DLUsability/JCDL02.html.

Leazer, G. H., Gilliland-Swetland, A. J. and Borgman, C. L. (2000) Evaluating the Use of a Geographic Digital Library in Undergraduate Classrooms: ADEPT. In *Proceedings of the 5th ACM Conference on Digital Libraries, San Antonio, Texas, ACM, New York, NY*, 248–49.

Leazer, G. H., Gilliland-Swetland, A. J., Borgman, C. L. and Mayer, R. E. (2000) Classroom Evaluation of the Alexandria Digital Earth Prototype (ADEPT). In *Proceedings of the American Society for Information Science 2000 Annual Conference, ASIS, Chicago, IL*, 334–40, http://is.gseis.ucla.edu/adept/pubs/asisadept.htm.

Liew, C. L. (2005) Cross-Cultural Design and Usability of a Digital Library Supporting Access to Maori Cultural Heritage Resources. In Theng, Y.-L. and Foo, S. (eds), *Design and Usability of Digital Libraries: case studies in the Asia-Pacific*, Information Science Publishing, 284–97.

Madle, G., Kostkova, P., Mani-Saada, J. and Weinberg, J. (2003) *Development of a Methodology to Evaluate the Impact of a Medical Digital Library on User Knowledge, Attitude and Behaviour*, www.hon.ch/Mednet2003/abstracts/491753869.html.

Maly, K., Nelson, M., Shen, S., Zeil, S. and Zubair, M. (n.d.) *Digital Library for Undergraduate Science Education Evaluation Framework*, http://dlib.cs.odu.edu/ completed-projects/ndif/nsf/ dlib2/udifplan/evaluationframework/evaluation.doc.

Marchionini, G. (2000) Evaluating Digital Libraries: a longitudinal and multifaceted view, *Library Trends*, **49** (2), 304–33.

Marchionini, G. and Komlodi, A. (1998) Design of Interfaces for Information Seeking, *Annual Review of Information Science and Technology*, **33**, 89–130.

Meyyappan, N., Chowdhury, G. G. and Foo, S. (2001) Use of a Digital Work Environment (DWE) Prototype to Create a User-Centred University Digital Library, *Journal of Information Science*, **27** (4), 249–64.

Meyyappan, N., Foo, S. and Chowdhury, G. G. (2004) Design of a Task-Based Digital Library for the Academic Community, *Journal of Documentation*, **60** (4), 449–75.

Nicholas, D., Huntington, P. and Williams, P. (2003) Micro-Mining Log Files: a method for enriching the data yield from internet log files, *Journal of Information Science*, **29**, summer, 391–404.

Nielsen, J. and Levy, J. (1994) Measuring Usability Preference vs Performance, *Communications of the ACM*, **37** (4), 66–76.

Norlin, E. (2000) Reference Evaluation: a three-step approach-surveys, unobtrusive observations, and focus groups, *College and Research Libraries*, **61** (6), 546–53.

Pan, B., Gay, G., Saylor, J., Hembrooke, H. and Henderson, D. (2004) Usability, Learning, and Subjective Experience: user evaluation of K-MODDL in an undergraduate class. In *Proceedings of the 2004 Joint ACM/IEEE Conference on Digital Libraries, Tucson, Arizona, ACM, New York, NY*, 188–89.

Park, S. (2000) Usability, User Preferences, Effectiveness, and User Behaviours When Searching Individual and Integrated Full-Text Databases: implications for digital libraries, *Journal of the American Society for Information Science*, **51** (5), 456–68.

Peng, L. K., Ramaiah, C. K. and Foo, S. (2004) Heuristic-Based User Interface Evaluation at Nanyang Technological University in Singapore, *Program*, **38** (1), 42–59.

Sandusky, R. J. (2002) Digital Library Attributes: framing usability research. In Blandford, A. and Buchanan, G. (eds), *JCDL'02 Workshop on Usability of Digital Libraries*, 5–7, www.uclic.ucl.ac.uk/annb/DLUsability/JCDL02.html.

Skykes, J., Dobreva, M., Birrell, D., McCulloch, E., Ruthven, I., Ünal, Y. and Feliciati, P. (2010) Focus on End Users: eye-tracking analysis for digital libraries. In Lalmas, M. et al. (eds), *Research and Advanced Technology for Digital Libraries, 14th European Digital Library Conference, Glasgow, 14–16 Sept*, Lecture Notes in Computer Science 6273, 510–13.

Stelmaszewska, H. and Blandford, A. (2002) *Patterns of Interactions: user behaviour in response to search results*, www.uclic.ucl.ac.uk/annb/DLUsability/Stelmaszewska29.pdf.

Sumner, T. (2005) Report on the 5th ACM/IEEE Joint Conference on Digital Libraries – cyberinfrastructure for research and education, *D-Lib Magazine*, **11** (7/8), www.dlib.org/dlib/july05/sumner/07sumner.html.

Sumner, T. and Marlino, M. (2004) Digital Libraries and Educational Practice: a case for new models, *Proceedings of JCDL '04, Tucson, Arizona, 7–11 June*, 170–8.

9

The digital divide, digital natives and usability

Introduction

The distinction between those who have access to information and communication technologies (ICTs) and those who do not is called the digital divide. It marks the disparity between ICT 'haves' and 'have nots'. At first the digital divide was defined in binary terms: a gap between ICT 'haves' and 'have nots', but more recently researchers (Norris, 2001; Chowdhury, 2004) have noted that a digital divide can be of different types:

- *the social divide*: the difference in access between diverse social groups
- *the global divide*: the difference in access to the internet
- *the democratic divide*: the different applications and uses of online information to engage and participate in social life.

There is a general belief that the digital divide only exists between the developed and developing counties. While this is true – because of the lack of ICT infrastructure, telephone and internet access, and generally poor educational level and socio-economic conditions of the population in developing countries – a digital divide also exists among different sectors of societies in developed countries.

How does the digital divide affect usability of information products and services? Obviously if people have no or only limited access to ICTs in general, and internet and digital information services in particular, they will use no online information products and services, or fewer than others do. This chapter discusses the concept of the digital divide, how it is measured, and associated parameters such as digital literacy. It provides some statistics to indicate how the digital divide exists in different nations in the developed and developing world, and discusses how the digital divide affects the usability of information products and services and what lessons can be learned relating to digital literacy research.

Connotations of the digital divide

In a report on the digital divide the Organisation for Economic Co-operation and Development (OECD) (2001) defines the digital divide as 'the gap between individuals, households, businesses and geographic areas at different socio-economic levels with regard to their opportunities to access information and communication technologies (ICTs) and to their use of the internet for a wide variety of activities. The digital divide reflects various differences among and within countries.' The report identifies the most important indicators of the digital divide as computer and internet availability, and availability of alternative access to information through TVs or mobile phones. According to the OECD (2001), the digital divide in households depends primarily on income and education. Other variables of the digital divide – household size and type, age, gender, racial and linguistic background and location – also play an important role.

Thus availability of ICT infrastructure and access are not the only determinant factors of a digital divide. It may be influenced by a host of other socio-economic factors such as difference in age, gender, level of education, geographic location, ethnicity, language skill and socio-economic structure. Gurstein (2003) argued that other factors influencing the digital divide are political and self-decision. As stated in the introduction, most digital divide research in the past focused on the difference between internet 'haves' and 'have nots', but more recently research has investigated further differences (DiMaggio et al., 2004). Recent research (Webster, 2006; Van Dijck, 2009; Brandtzaeg, 2010; Hargittai, 2010) focuses on other factors that influence the digital divide, such as the imbalance of internet use, variability of users' capability, and how similar levels of access engage users in different ways. Some researchers (Vicente Cuervo and Lopez Menedez, 2006) show that the multiple dimensions of the digital divide are related to ICT infrastructure and use as well as costs and the availability of online public services. Vicente Cuervo and Lopez Menedez (2006) showed that the disparity of the digital divide is due to social and economic differences across countries.

Roe (2006) said that 'despite confident millennial predictions of its inevitable and inexorable demise, the digital divide . . . is very much with us'.

When reviewing digital divide research and its achievements and shortcomings between 2000 and 2005, Van Dijk (2006) pointed out that digital divide research has identified four types of access: physical, skills, motivational and usage. The digital divide relating to physical access seems to be closing in the most developed countries, but the divide relating to digital skills and the use of applications persists or widens. Usage access has dominated research most in recent years (Morey, 2007; Valadez and Durán, 2007; Hargittai 2010; Brandtzaeg, Heim and Karahasanovic, 2011).

Indicators of the digital divide

Gurstein (2003) argued that effective use of ICTs transforms one's economic, social, cultural and political condition significantly, so attention should be given to providing access to these technologies. The Asian Development Bank (ADB) (2007) recognized that ICTs can help close the digital divide by providing economically feasible, inclusive access to information and services designed to help children learn, adults enhance skills and organizations reach across barriers to connect those in need.

Drori (2010) suggested that closing the global digital divide depends on the basic conditions of ICT access and e-literacy, but the notion of the digital divide is complex and multidimensional. Earlier (2005) he observed that it is influenced by factors like gender, wealth and education, race and ethnicity, whereas the global digital divide between countries is influenced by national wealth, literacy and democracy. The OECD's Directorate of Science and Technology and Industry (DSTI; www.oecd.org) identifies the following key indicators that can be used to assess the extent of the digital divide within and among countries:

- access lines and access paths in total and per 100 inhabitants
- mobile subscribers in total and per 100 inhabitants
- internet subscribers in total
- broadband subscribers per 100 inhabitants
- availability of digital subscriber lines in the country
- cable TV subscribers in total
- the number of households with access to a home computer
- the number of households with access to the internet
- the number of households with access to broadband
- the extent of internet penetration by size or class of population

- percentage of businesses with ten or more employees using the internet
- the extent of internet selling and purchasing by industry
- the extent of business use of broadband
- the share of ICT-related occupations in the total economy
- telecommunication services revenue
- mobile telecommunication services revenue in total
- telecommunication infrastructure investment in total
- the share of ICT value added in the business sector value added
- R&D expenditure in selected ICT industries
- the share of ICT employment in business sector employment
- ICT-related patents as a percentage of national total patent filings
- the share of countries in ICT-related patents filed
- top 50 telecommunications firms and IT firms
- the contribution of ICT-using services to value added per person engaged
- the contribution of ICT investment to GDP growth.

A closer look at the list shows that each of these factors has significant implications on the usability of information products and services. Figure 9.1 shows the ICT indicators identified by the OECD for an information society and therefore the ICT indicators for the digital divide.

Digital divide indicators and usability

Data relating to the two key indicators of the digital divide – home computer and internet and broadband use in selected countries – are presented in Figures 9.2, 9.3 and 9.4 on the following pages.

It may be noted that out of the 35 countries listed in Figure 9.4 only seven (20%) countries have 80% or more households with both home computer and internet connection. However, only two out of 35 countries have more than 80% households with a broadband internet connection. Only about two-thirds of the 27 EU countries have a broadband connection at home, and in many European countries like the Czech Republic, Portugal, Italy and Greece less than 50% households have a broadband connection.

In the USA only just over 60% households have a broadband internet connection, so more than a third of the country's households do not yet have a broadband internet connection. A recent US government report (NTIA, 2010) outlines the current state of the digital divide in the USA, and the reasons behind lower usage of internet from home, as follows:

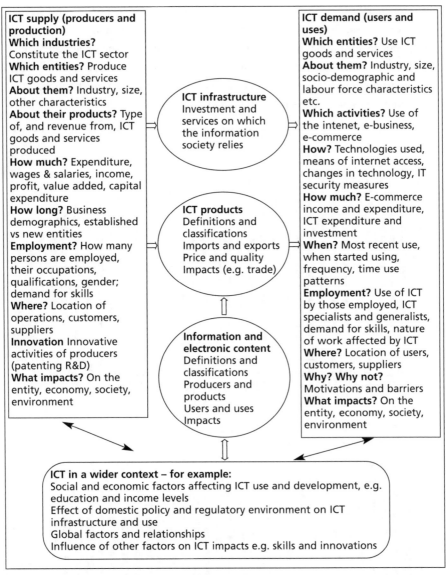

Figure 9.1 *ICT indicators for an information society and digital divide (OECD, 2008)*

Despite the growing importance of the Internet in American life, over 30 percent of households and 35 percent of persons do not use the Internet at home, and 30 percent of all persons do not use the Internet anywhere. Those with no broadband access at home amount to more than 35 percent of all households and approximately 40 percent of all persons, with a larger proportion in rural areas in both categories. Overall, the two most important reasons given by survey respondents for not having broadband access at home are 'don't need' and 'too expensive.' Inadequate or no computer is also a major reason given for no home broadband adoption. In rural America, lack of availability is a much more important reason for non-adoption than in urban areas.

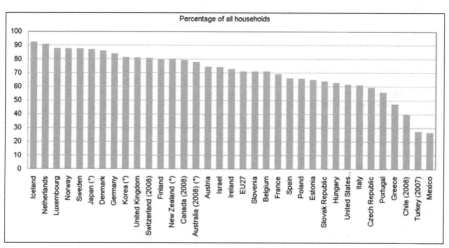

Figure 9.2   *Households with access to a computer at home, 2009 or latest available year (%) (OECD and Eurostat, 2010a)*

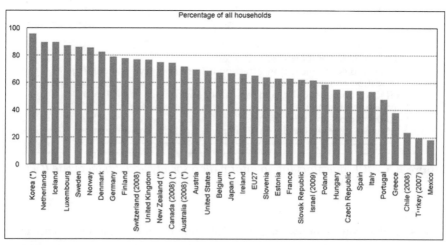

Figure 9.3   *Households with access to the internet, 2009 or latest available year (%) (OECD and Eurostat, 2010b)*

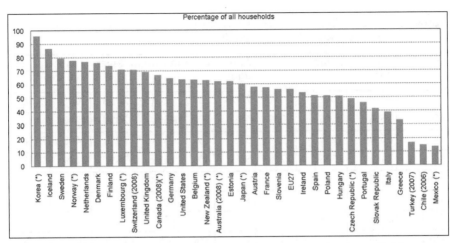

Figure 9.4   *Households with broadband access, 2009 or latest available year (%) (OECD and Eurostat, 2010c)*

In the UK about 70% households have a broadband connection. Recent government statistics show that in 2010, 30.1 million adults (60%) in the UK accessed the internet every day or almost every day (www.statistics.gov.uk/). When asked why their household did not have an internet connection (Table 9.1), respondents' most common reply was that they didn't need it (39%), followed by those who said a lack of skills prevented them from having the internet (21%).

Table 9.1 *Reason for UK household not having internet, 2010 (ONS, 2010)*	
Don't need it	39%
Lack of skills	21%
Don't want it	20%
Equipment costs too high	18%
Access costs too high	15%
Have access to internet elsewhere	8%
Privacy or security concerns	4%
Physical disability	2%
Base: UK households without internet access	

Table 9.2 overleaf shows that the last use of the internet varied depending on the age of respondents, especially for those aged 65+: 60% of people in the 65+ age group had never used the internet, which may be 18% of the total population (ONS, 2010). Thus a large proportion of the 18% user population

Table 9.2 *When adults in the UK last used the internet, by sex and age group, 2008–2010 (ONS, 2010)*

	Within the last 3 months			More than 3 months ago			Never used it		
	2008	2009	2010	2008	2009	2010	2008	2009	2010
Men	75%	80%	79%	4%	3%	5%	20%	17%	16%
Women	66%	72%	75%	5%	4%	4%	29%	24%	21%
All	71%	76%	77%	5%	4%	4%	25%	21%	18%
Age									
16–24	93%	96%	97%	5%	3%	2%	1%	3%	1%
25–44	87%	92%	93%	5%	3%	3%	8%	5%	4%
45–54	78%	81%	84%	4%	3%	4%	17%	16%	11%
55–64	63%	72%	72%	4%	4%	6%	33%	24%	22%
65+	26%	30%	32%	5%	5%	7%	70%	64%	60%
Base: UK adults									

who have never used the internet before is the 65+ age group. These figures are very useful for information professionals from the information product design and usability points of view because they provide an idea of which percentage of the population use or do not use the internet and thus how an information product or service targeted for a specific age group of gender has to be designed or modified.

As Figures 9.2, 9.3 and 9.4 show, countries like Turkey, Chile and Mexico have less than 20% households with a broadband internet connection. Even in some developed EU countries like Italy, Spain and Ireland 50% or more households still do not have a broadband connection. Overall there is only a handful of countries where 80% or more households have a broadband internet connection and a home computer. Thus most countries in the world, including the UK and USA, have a long way to go to bridge the digital divide when measured by the extent of computer and internet access. The gap is greatest between those in the lead, like South Korea, Iceland and the Scandinavian countries, and those that trail behind, like Mexico, Chile, Turkey, Greece and Italy.

The digital divide and digital natives

Prensky (2001) observed that there is also a digital divide between generations, such as 'digital natives' and 'digital immigrants', resulting from differences in technology use and skills. He distinguished between digital natives, who are 'native speakers' of the digital language of computers, video games and the internet and for whom these are integral parts of their lives; and digital immigrants, who were not born into the digital world but have at some point in their life become fascinated by and adopted many or most aspects of the new technology. As a result of this ubiquitous digital environment, today's students and younger generation think and process information fundamentally differently from their predecessors (Richter, Anderson-Inman and Frisbee, 2007; Palfrey and Gasser, 2008):

- They prefer multitasking and instant access to information.
- They live in the age of the Web 2.0 world where social networking and text messaging are the preferred channels for sharing and communicating ideas.
- They want learning that is fast-paced, multimedia, multimodal, interactive and digital.

However, Bennett, Maton and Kervin (2008) argued that digital natives may know how to use the internet and mobile technology, but they lack a critical understanding of the media. Other researchers (Rowlands et al., 2008, Hargittai, 2010) concur and do not support the idea that young adults are universally knowledgeable about the web.

The Centre for Information Behaviour and the Evaluation of Research (CIBER) at University College London has systematically analysed the literature on young people's use of new technology over 30 years and conducted an intergenerational experiment to see how people of different ages used educational web resources (CIBER, n.d.). These are CIBER's key findings:

- The information literacy of young people has not improved with the widening access to technology.
- The speed of young people's web searching means that little time is spent in evaluating information for relevance, accuracy or authority.
- Young people have a poor understanding of their information needs and thus find it difficult to develop effective search strategies.
- They exhibit a strong preference for expressing themselves in natural language rather than analysing which key words might be more useful.

Cunningham (2010) observed that digital natives are now making their way into the workplace, and, having grown up alongside the technology, they have a different understanding and expectations of technology in a business environment from digital migrants. It is therefore important for digital natives to learn how to make 'effective use' of information to close the digital divide. Waycott et al. (2010) argued that a better understanding of the use of technology for a particular purpose and the implications of technology for higher education is needed, but information literacy levels vary significantly within and across generations (New Media Consortium, 2007). Therefore, 'growing information literacy levels will mean that electronic provision of information and learning must become more sophisticated and utilise the applications and techniques that draw young people to online systems already' (Gunter, Rowlands and Nicholas, 2009).

Information skills and usability

While improved access to ICT and the internet are important for all sorts of reasons, one should not think that computers, networks or the internet can alone solve all the problems. Merely having access to ICT and the internet does not mean that these technologies will be used appropriately to access information and knowledge for solving problems, or for education, learning and research.

In order to make optimum use of ICT and the internet to obtain access to and use appropriate information for day-to-day activities, work or learning, people need to acquire the competencies and skills necessary to take advantage of these technologies. Norris (2001) suggested that the digital divide or online inequalities should be assessed according to users' degree of access to the technology and their information skills. Nielsen (2006) stressed that technology plays a major role in the digital divide as it is not enough to have computers and internet connections if users do not know how to benefit from them. He pointed out that almost 40% of the population has lower than average literacy skills and lower literacy is the web's biggest accessibility issue.

Warschauer (2003) commented that 'technology does not exist as an external variable to be injected from the outside to bring about certain results'. Better access to the appropriate ICT and the internet may provide access to information resources, but it is still necessary to find the most appropriate information relevant to solve a problem. This is one of the major challenges for today's information product or service designers and researchers. Gunter, Rowlands and Nicholas (2009) argued that educational systems have an important part to play in achieving this objective by using ICTs in ways that establish them as normative information resources and imparting the skills needed to use them fully.

Context and the digital divide

As discussed earlier in this book (especially in Chapter 3) information needs of users are influenced by the nature of their work, affiliation, educational background, accessibility to technology, and so on. Users face a number of problems in today's digital environment:

- They do not know which information source may be appropriate to accomplish a particular task or to resolve a specific problem.
- Even if users are aware of the existence of a particular information source, they may not know how to locate it, retrieve the information and make effective use of it.

A one-stop window approach, with facilities for task-based organization and access, personalization and automatic filtering based on user characteristics and tasks, may bring the solution. Europeana (www.europeana.eu) is an example in this context. It is a digital library for researchers, professionals and the public giving a single access point to Europe's cultural heritage linking up to databases all over Europe. The website (Europeana, n.d.) states, 'Europeana enables people to explore the digital resources of Europe's museums, libraries, archives and audio-visual collections. It promotes discovery and networking opportunities in a multilingual space where users can engage, share in and be inspired by the rich diversity of Europe's cultural and scientific heritage.' So, in addition to being a one-stop shop for access to Europe's cultural heritage, Europeana is a virtual space for community engagement for accessing, using and sharing Europe's cultural heritage information in multilingual virtual space. However, as Figure 9.4 shows, there is unequal broadband access across European and other countries. Will the use of Europeana be affected by this digital divide or can it diminish the digital divide between different people's access to and use of information? It is still a big challenge to information professionals.

Brandtzaeg, Heim and Karahasanovic (2011) showed there is a new digital divide, a 'user type divide', where imbalance of internet usage or online participation is the key factor to understand the new digital divide. They observed that 60% of European citizens from the countries investigated lag alarmingly behind others in their internet usage, out of which 42% are non-users and 18% are sporadic users. The study predicted the presence of a 'rich get richer' effect in which the divide between the different user types will increase in connection with the growing development and distribution of the internet and its technologies.

Summary

The discussion so far in this chapter indicates that the digital divide is a complex phenomenon: it depends on a number of technical, social and personal factors, and it is a moving target. In some areas the digital divide is closing, but in others the gap widens or persists especially in relation to the effective and efficient use of information. Stern (2010) observed that knowledge-intensive activities are a critical part of the modern knowledge-based economy and sadly access to and proficiency with information and communication technologies are not shared equally within and between countries.

Digital literacy skills play an important role along with other factors in internet access and use. The New Media Consortium (2011) noted: 'Although there is broad consensus that digital media literacy is vitally important for today's students, what skills constitute digital literacy are still not well defined nor universally taught.' Therefore, it is a big challenge to an information professional in the twenty-first century. Ferro, Helbig and Gil-Garcia (2011) suggested that the 'digital divide is best understood, managed and tackled in context'. With regard to the design of information products and services for digital natives and digital immigrants, differences between the technologies used in daily life and those used in education and for different types of activities should be understood within the specific user context.

As discussed in Chapter 8, digital library research and development have grown fast over the past 20 or so years, and in that process many digital libraries and digital information products and services have appeared. The focus originally was to develop enabling technologies to design and build digital libraries with distributed collections of digital resources in different forms and formats. Subsequently, researchers have shifted their focus on users, usability and impact studies. However, bridging the digital divide is a necessary condition for achieving the goals of digital library research and development (Chowdhury, 2004). Improved access to ICT, the internet and other modes of access to information, and adherence to web accessibility guidelines and standards (as discussed in Chapter 7), are important for promoting access to digital content. Øverby and Hypatia (2007) commented that accessibility to ICT systems and digital content should be considered an important aspect of the global challenge to close the digital divide.

As discussed in this chapter, contrary to popular belief, researchers show that some digital natives, despite being ICT and internet savvy, suffer from information illiteracy – lacking the skills required to find the right information for the right job with minimum effort – just as some of their digital immigrant counterparts do. This brings new challenges for information product and service designers as well as for academic institutions for improving the information skills of the younger generation. David Nicol, deputy director of the Centre for Academic Practice and Learning Enhancement at the University of Strathclyde, was quoted in Fearn (2008): 'It's not just about using the tools, it's about using the tools effectively. We've got to bridge the gap between informal learning using digital technology and formal learning in the institution.' Sir David Melville (former Vice-chancellor of the University of Kent), also quoted in Fearn (2008), added: 'Students lack those critical skills. They have got used to getting huge amounts of material in this way, but not very critically.'

Yamazaki (2007) stressed that the role of information professionals will be indispensable with the ability of efficient communication, basic knowledge of business processes and literacy on computers and networks, and that information professionals 'are expected to be leaders like conductors of symphony orchestras to carry all the members working together to a single goal'. Chowdhury (2004) and Chowdhury and Chowdhury (2008) suggested that one possible approach to improving the usability of information products and services may be to build a layer on top of the existing array of web and digital library services that can be user-centred and hide all the complexities of each individual system and service. Flexible, portable and scalable design layers, something like the digital work environment designed by Chowdhury and his associates (Meyyappan, Chowdhury and Foo, 2001a, 2001b, 2001c; Meyyappan, Foo and Chowdhury, 2004), may be built and used to improve usability of digital library services. Other examples of usability studies, for example Dobreva and Chowdhury (2010), resulting in improved product design, may be the new annotation tools for researchers that may be added to Europeana in response to user demand.

References

ADB (2007) *South Asia Economic Report: social sectors in transition*, Asian Development Bank, www.adb.org/Documents/Reports/Social-Sectors-Transition/socialsectorstransition.pdf.

Bennett, S., Maton, K. and Kervin, L. (2008) The 'Digital Natives' Debate: a critical review of the evidence, *British Journal of Educational Technology*, **39** (5), 775–86.

Brandtzaeg, P. B. (2010) Towards a Unified Media-User-Typology (MUT): a meta-analysis and review of the research literature on media-user typologies, *Computers in Human Behaviour*, **26** (5), 940–56.

Brandtzaeg, P. B., Heim, J. and Karahasanovic, A. (2011) Understanding the New Digital Divide – a typology of internet users in Europe, *International Journal of Human-Computer Studies*, **69**, 123–38.

Chowdhury, G. G. (2004) Access to Information in Digital Libraries: users and digital divide, paper presented at the *International Conference on Digital Libraries*, New Delhi, 24–27 February.

Chowdhury, G. G. and Chowdhury, S. (2008) SIMLIS: a student-centred information management to support learning and living of LIS students in HEIs, *8th HEA Annual Conference*, Southampton, August.

CIBER (n.d.) Google Generation Research at University College London, www.ucl.ac.uk/infostudies/research/ciber/GG2.pdf.

Cunningham, J. (2010) New Workers, New Workplace?: getting the balance right, *Strategic Direction*, **26** (1), 5–6.

DiMaggio, P., Hargittai, E., Celesta, C. and Shafer, S. (2004) Digital Inequality: from unequal access to differentiated use. In Neckerman, K. (ed.), *Social Inequality*, Russell Sage, 355–400.

Dobreva, M. and Chowdhury, S. (2010) A User-Centric Evaluation of the Europeana Digital Library. In *The Role of Digital Libraries in a Time of Global Change*, *[Proceedings of the] 12th International Conference on Asia-Pacific Digital Libraries*, *ICADL 2010, Gold Coast, Australia, June 21–25*, Lecture Notes in Computer Science Series 6102, Springer, 148–57.

Drori, G. S. (2005) *Global E-litism: digital technology, social inequality, and transnationality*, Worth Publishers.

Drori, G. S. (2010) Globalization and Technology Divides: bifurcation of policy between the 'digital divide' and the 'innovative divide', *Sociological Inquiry*, **80** (1), 63–91.

Europeana (n.d.) *Europeana: think culture*, www.europeana.eu/portal/aboutus.html.

Fearn, H. (2008) Grappling with the Digital Divide, *Times Higher Education*, 14 August, www.timeshighereducation.co.uk/story.asp?storycode=403135.

Ferro, E., Helbig, N. C. and Gil-Garcia, R. (2011) The Role of IT Literacy in Defining Digital Divide Policy Needs, *Government Information Quarterly*, **28**, 3–10.

Gunter, B., Rowlands, I. and Nicholas, D. (2009) *The Google Generation: are ICT innovations changing information-seeking behaviour?*, Chandos Publishing.

Gurstein, M. (2003) Effective Use: a community informatics strategy beyond the digital divide, *First Monday*, 8 (12), http://firstmonday.org/htbin/cgiwrap/bin/ojs/index.php/fm/article/viewArticle/110 7/1027.

Hargittai, E. (2010) Digital Na(t)ives? Variation in internet skills and uses among members of the 'net generation', *Sociological Inquiry*, **80** (1), 92–113.

Meyyappan, N., Chowdhury, G. G. and Foo, S. (2001a) An Architecture of a User-Centred Digital Library for the Academic Community. In Chen, C. C. (ed.), *Global Digital Library Development in the New Millennium: fertile ground for distributed cross-disciplinary collaboration*, Tsinghua University Press, 175–82.

Meyyappan, N., Chowdhury, G. G. and Foo, S. (2001b) Design and Development of a User-Centred Digital Library System: some basic guidelines. In Urs, S., Rajashekar, T. B. and Raghavan, K. S. (eds), *Digital Libraries: dynamic landscape for knowledge creation, access and management, the 4th International Conference of Asian Digital Libraries, Bangalore, 10–12 December*, 135–48.

Meyyappan, N., Chowdhury, G. G. and Foo, S. (2001c) Use of a Digital Work Environment (DWE) Prototype to Create a User-centred University Digital Library, *Journal of Information Science*, **27** (4), 249–64.

Meyyappan, N., Foo, S. and Chowdhury, G. G. (2004) Design and Evaluation of a Task-based Digital Library for the Academic Community, *Journal of Documentation*, **60** (4), 449–75.

Morey, O. T. (2007) Digital Disparities: the persistent digital divide as related to health information access on the internet, *Journal of Consumer Health on the Internet*, **11** (4), 23–41.

New Media Consortium (2007) *The Horizon Report*, New Media Consortium with EDUCAUSE Learning Initiative.

New Media Consortium (2011) *The Horizon Report*, www.nmc.org/pdf/2011-Horizon-Report.pdf.

Nielsen, J. (2006) *Digital Divide: the three stages, Jakob Nielsen's Alertbox*, www.useit.com/alertbox/digital-divide.html.

Norris, P. (2001) *Digital Divide: civic engagement, information poverty, and the internet worldwide*, Cambridge University Press.

NTIA (2010) *Digital Nation: 21st century America's progress toward universal broadband internet access*, National Telecommunications and Information Administration, www.ntia.doc.gov/reports/2010/NTIA_internet_use_report_Feb2010.pdf.

OECD (2001) *Understanding the Digital Divide*, www.oecd.org/dataoecd/38/57/1888451.pdf.

OECD (2008) *Measuring the Impacts of ICT Using Official Statistics*, Directorate for Science Technology and Industry, Committee for Information, Computer and Communications Policy, DSTI/ICCP/IIS(2007)1/FINAL.

OECD and Eurostat (2010a) Households with Access to a Computer at Home, 2009 or Latest Available Year. In *Community Survey on ICT Usage in Households and by Individuals*, www.oecd.org/dataoecd/19/46/34083096.xls.

OECD and Eurostat (2010b) Households with Access to the Internet, 2009 or Latest Available Year. In *Community Survey on ICT Usage in Households and by Individuals*, www.oecd.org/dataoecd/19/45/34083073.xls.

OECD and Eurostat (2010c) Households with Broadband Access, 2009 or Latest Available Year. In *Community Survey on ICT Usage in Households and by Individuals*, www.oecd.org/dataoecd/23/34/41625794.xls.

ONS (2010) Internet Access 2010: households and individuals, *ONS Statistical Bulletin*, 27 August, Office for National Statistics, www.statistics.gov.uk/pdfdir/iahi0810.pdf.

Øverby, E. and Hypatia, A. (2007) *Bridging the Accessibility Divide to Digital Information*, IEEE GIIS 2007 Symposium, 4–6.

Palfrey, J. and Gasser, U. (2008) *Born Digital: understanding the first generation of digital natives*, Basic Books.

Prensky, M. (2001) Digital Natives, Digital Immigrants, *On the Horizon*, **9** (5).

Richter, J., Anderson-Inman, L. and Frisbee, M. (2007) Critical Engagement of Teachers, Second Life: progress in the Salamander Project, www.cis.paisley.ac.uk/livi-ci0/slccedu2007rev2.doc.

Roe, K. (2006) The Digital Divide in the Twenty-First Century: an introduction, editorial, *Poetics*, **34**, 219–20.

Rowlands, I., Nicholas, D., Williams, P., Huntington, P. and Fieldhouse, M. (2008) The Google Generation: the information behaviour of the researcher of the future, *Aslib Proceedings: New Information Perspectives*, **60** (4), 209–310.

Stern, M. J. (2010) Inequality in the Internet Age: a twenty-first century dilemma, *Sociological Inquiry*, **80** (1), 28–33.

Valadez, J. R. and Durán, R. P. (2007) Redefining the Digital Divide: beyond access to computers and the internet, *High School Journal*, **90** (3), 31–44.

Van Dijck, J. D. (2009) Wikinomics and its Discontents: a critical analysis of Wen 2.0 business manifesto, *New Media & Society*, **11** (5), 855–74.

Van Dijk, J. A. G. M. (2006) Digital Divide Research, Achievements and Shortcomings, *Poetics*, **34**, 221–35.

Vicente Cuervo, M. R. and Lopez Menendez, A J. (2006) A Multivariate Framework for the Analysis of the Digital Divide: evidence for the European Union-15, *Information & Management*, **43**, 756–66.

Warschauer, M. (2003) Demystifying the digital divide, *Scientific American*, **289** (2), 42.

Waycott, J., Bennett, S., Kennedy, G., Dalgarno, B. and Gray, K. (2010) Digital Divides? Student and staff perceptions of information and communication technologies, *Computers & Education*, **54**, 1202–11.

Webster, F. (2006) *Theories of Information Society*, Routledge.

Yamazaki, H. (2007) Changing Society, Role of Information Professional and Strategy for Libraries, *IFLA Journal*, **33** (1), 50–8.

10

Issues and trends in usability research

Introduction

Although general evaluation and performance measurements of library and information services, and evaluation of information online information services and databases have a long history, usability studies of information websites and online information products and services are of recent origin. Methods, tools and technologies that have been developed and used within software communities – the human–computer interaction community in particular – and subsequently in the context of the web have been adopted for usability research in the context of online information products and services. However, since users are at the core of any usability study and user studies have remained a major area of research within the information science community, many methods and techniques that were developed for user studies have been adopted and used in usability research. While significant amounts of progress have been made to usability research in information, many new challenges have also appeared over the past few years. Some of these challenges result from the changing nature of the web and emerging technologies, standards and so on; others are caused by the very nature of the web and ICTs that are affected by many factors, including the digital divide, digital and information literacy and the fast changing nature of society caused by the culture of web and mobile technologies, social networking technologies and so on. These emerging technologies and culture bring tremendous opportunities as well as challenges for usability researchers within the information science community. This chapter provides a quick overview of some of the emerging technologies and challenges and points out some new research to show the trends and opportunities in usability research.

Usability methods and techniques

As discussed earlier in this book, usability studies in digital libraries and online information products and services use a variety of methods and techniques, most of which were originally developed within the software engineering and human–computer interaction research communities. However, some tools and techniques, such as transaction log analysis, eye tracking and cognitive studies of users, are of relatively recent origin and have been adopted from other fields of studies. Similarly, other areas of study and corresponding methods and techniques, such as in the digital divide, information literacy and so on, are being brought within usability research since they have a significant impact on the usability of online information products and services.

Earlier studies, for example Jones, Zenios and Griffiths (2004), pointed out that disciplinary and subject differences have a significant influence on the usability of digital libraries. Borgman et al. (2005) reported that searching by concept is essential but difficult because of the different ways in which data and images can be interpreted and used in a digital library environment. Chowdhury (2004) highlighted a number of usability problems currently facing digital library users. In the digital library world, the onus is still on users to decide where to look for a specific item of information, and to consolidate the results retrieved from heterogeneous systems. This is often the biggest problem in information access. A number of researchers – see for example Meyyappan, Chowdhury and Foo (2001), Chowdhury (2004), Meyyappan, Foo and Chowdhury (2004) and Borgman et al. (2005) – have highlighted the importance of personal digital libraries and suggested that a personal digital library could help users. When reporting on academics' use of the Alexandria Digital Library, Borgman et al. (2005) suggested that each user needs his or her own personal space in which to manage digital objects; some of the personal digital library content may be selected from a shared space; other content will be imported from personal collections of research and teaching resources.

Chowdhury (2004) recommended a task-based information access system and a one-stop window for accessing digital libraries where the user will not have to spend time on deciding where and how to search for the required information; instead, the user may just specify a task on hand, and the system would then perform the search and recommend a set of information resources suitable for accomplishing the chosen task. Progress towards this can be seen in projects such as MIND, which developed tools for resource selection and data fusion; see Gibb (2002) and Wu, Crestani and Gibb (2004).

While such a system may be useful, digital library designers may adapt systems that are prevalent in the web environment.

There are many web aggregator services that, given a set of user requirements, gather, filter and present information relevant to users' needs. Aggregator services have been in existence in the information world for some time, but they only do part of the job compared with web aggregator services. For example online services such as Dialog are aggregators that provide access to a range of online databases through one search interface, and consolidate the results based on system or user-defined criteria. Similarly services like ProQuest give their users access to a range of electronic resources drawn from several e-journals and databases. While they are good services, in the digital library world users often find it difficult to decide which source to select and search, and the problem is compounded by the different search features and facilities offered by the services.

Over the past few years, a number of personalization and recommendation systems and services have been introduced that aim to improve the usability of information services by retrieving information to meet specific user needs, and filtering out unwanted information; see for example Hicks, 2003; Anand and Mobasher, 2005; Fan, Gordon and Pathak, 2005; Renda and Straccia, 2005; Frias-Martinez et al., 2006. Shahabi and Chen (2003) observed that these systems are not without flaws, and Anand and Mobasher (2005) commented that 'most personalization systems tend to use a static profile of the user; however, user interests are not static, changing with time and context'; only a number of systems attempted to handle the dynamics within the user profile (McCallum and Nigam, 1998; Billsus and Pazzani, 2000; Koychev and Schwab, 2000). A better solution would be to adopt a service like those provided by web aggregators, where users would only need to specify their information need, or more specifically the task or a profile, and the system would take care of the rest of the process.

In more recent years, researchers at University College London have used deep log analysis techniques to understand user behaviour and usability of online information products such as e-books. JISC (2007) noted: 'Deep log analysis is a methodology that helps librarians, publishers and other suppliers of web-based content to a better understanding of how consumers actually use their services.' The key findings of the e-book observatory project (JISC, 2009), a first-time large-scale national study of e-book usability in the UK, touch on a number of key areas of usability of digital content in general and e-books in particular:

- Nearly 65% of academics and students have used an e-book for their work, study or leisure, which indicates that e-books are becoming part of academic users' life and work.
- More than half of users' first access to e-books was through the library, and therefore libraries are a key player in the e-book market.
- Usage of course textbooks varies at different times of the year, often by as much as 50% from month to month.
- E-books were seen as a convenience and suitable for the students' busy lifestyles.
- Use of some platforms was compromised by technical and other barriers.
- Most students use e-books for fact finding, for example in encyclopaedias and dictionaries.
- A small group of 'super users' was identified who tend to seek and use e-books more actively and frequently.
- E-book platforms and interfaces are far from ideal; user-centred design principles need to be adopted to improve their quality and accessibility.
- The business models prevailing in the current e-book market are overly complex and often inappropriate for the target communities.
- Students from different disciplines access and use e-books in different ways: they were popular in business studies, but much less so in engineering; there were also differences in use depending on users' age and gender.
- Users are confused with the current access systems where they have to move from one platform to another; a one-window access through a single index would be preferable.
- Current methods of access to e-books via a link from the library catalogue were found inadequate; it was felt that discovery of e-books should be supported by promotion and marketing.

These and a host of other findings of the e-books observatory project provide a lot of valuable information on the usability of e-books in academic settings in UK higher education. They also clearly indicate how a well planned log analysis study can generate many useful findings on the usability of online information products and services that can be generalized for a user population at the national level.

Saulnier and Viaud (2009) conducted an expert heuristic evaluation of the Europeana Digital Library using a combination of:

- Nielsen heuristics (Nielsen, 1993), most widely used in ergonomics
- Rosenfeld heuristics (http://louisrosenfeld.com), which specialize more on the search interfaces of a website
- some directives of the W3C on web content accessibility
- some heuristics of the Centre de recherche informatique de Montréal (CRIM; www.crim.ca/en/).

They noted that in general the Europeana site complies with ergonomic rules based on the chosen sets of heuristics. While this heuristic evaluation was carried out by two experts, a more recent evaluation study (Dobreva and Chowdhury, 2010) involved a team of researchers from different countries and used multiple methods for data collection using focus groups and eye tracking experiments with participants from different countries and different sites. The second set of usability studies (Skykes et al., 2010) made 24 recommendations on content, functionality and navigation, and the eye tracking study was particularly useful for interface design and navigation issues.

External factors affecting usability

As discussed in Chapter 9, several external factors, especially the growing ICT and internet infrastructure and facilities relating to the digital divide, have a significant impact on usability of information products and services.

An OECD report (2008) warned that the fast developments of ICT and internet technologies will have negative and positive impacts on information access and use:

- Further expansion of broadband technology and its uses will facilitate social and productivity improvements from services in e-commerce, e-banking, e-government, e-education and e-health.
- Software advancements will take place in a number of areas, especially enhancement of ICT security, improved interoperability and portability of better data storage management, improved voice and image recognition capabilities, and improved knowledge-based applications.
- Further expansion of mobile phone and wireless technologies will offer the possibility of permanent connectivity via the internet, which will lead to further convergence of technologies: mobile phone and internet, internet and broadcasting, internet and phone and so on.

- Advances in ICT and internet technologies will be accompanied by malicious software and other security threats, such as attacks on critical information infrastructure, and therefore additional protection and security measures have to be developed.
- Radio frequency identification devices and similar sensor technologies have the potential to improve significantly the tracking of goods, vehicles, livestock and people, which will lead to better management of resources.

There will be new standards and policy guidelines to ensure better information systems design, access and management. Standards like web accessibility guidelines (discussed in Chapter 7) will improve usability of information products and services by ensuring that special access needs of people with disabilities and special needs are taken care of. Segev (2010) predicted that the digital divide of the future will be less about the technical difficulties of accessing the web, and less about the search engine capabilities of providing access to the deep web. The future digital divide will be more about the purposeful and deliberate organization, management and manipulation of information by different actors – information service providers, information system designers and more importantly businesses – in order to capture various sectors of the global market.

It is evident that the most innovative businesses in the information field, like Google, Microsoft and so on, will expand in breadth by providing access to some information useful to all users, and in depth by providing specific information and services for specific categories of users focusing on specific domains of science, technology, culture and so on. A new kind of digital divide may be created by the emerging business trends in the digital content market (discussed below) where dominant businesses like Amazon, Apple, Sony and so on divide the market with their own reading devices and specific licensing agreements for access to digital content. Parallel forces that may be able to reduce this divide are the open access and open scholarship movements, which aim to develop or adopt alternative business models for generating content with the main objective of making digital content available free at the point of use.

Emerging technologies for access to digital content

Publishers and booksellers have traditionally remained the main channels for direct purchase and access to content, and libraries, online databases and aggregator or search services have remained the main channels for social or shared access to content for a long time. This has changed recently and nowadays digital content can be accessed through a variety of channels and can be read using a variety of tools, from desktops and laptops to specifically designed reading devices and mobile phones.

Compared with e-journals, the popularity and adoption of e-books in academia has been slow, but many studies (for example, the Higher Education Consultancy Group, 2006, and Nicholas, Rowlands and Jamali, 2010) confirm that students and researchers now prefer digital books. The most prominent reason for preference of online materials over print is the ease of access. Citing data from SCONUL and the Association of Research Libraries, Bunkell and Dyas-Correia (2009) showed that the number of loans per volume for print books is very small at 0.18 to 1.3 accesses per volume per year, whereas the figure for digital books is 12–45 accesses per volume per year. Access to digital books in this context measures not only search but page viewing and/or downloading of content.

A variety of technology and business models have appeared since the late 2000s and as a result use of e-books in academic libraries has increased (see the next section for specific data) over the past few years. These are some examples of e-book business models prevailing in the higher education sector (for details see Bunkell and Dyas-Correia, 2009; Content Complete Ltd and OnlyConnect Consultancy, 2009; JISC, 2009; Pool, 2010):

- E-book collections are available from a number of major publishers such as Cambridge University Press, Elsevier, Oxford University Press, Palgrave, SAGE, Springer, Taylor & Francis and Wiley-Blackwell.
- Some textbooks are available to libraries by subscription or purchase as part of e-book collections offered by publishers and via aggregator platforms.
- In the USA the digital book market largely follows the 'student pays' model where digital versions of textbooks can be bought and downloaded to students' computers. CourseSmart is an example of this sort of software, with more than 6000 books available for student purchase.
- In the UK digital books are typically available only as part of print or e-book bundles from publishers, and in some cases with an additional payment from bookshop chains like John Smith and Son, where the

e-version is available for download via an access code supplied with the printed book.

- A number of aggregator services provide access to digital books from different publishers through one interface. Typical examples of such digital book aggregator services in the UK market include Dawson, EBL, ebrary, MyiLibrary and NetLibrary.
- Some online retailers, such as sellstudentstuff.com, ebooks.com and CourseSmart, in the USA offer download options to students for rental.
- Some publishers offer the option to purchase and download chapters of digital books as well as complete titles. Some publishers also offer print plus online or online-only access for specific periods of 3 to 12 months.
- Some publishers, for example Pearson and McGraw-Hill, offer lecturers the opportunity to create custom textbooks, and students can purchase the customized title in print or in a digital version.
- In some cases publishers provide supplementary e-resources that support adopted textbooks in pre-formatted 'cartridges' that institutions can upload into their virtual learning environment or make them available online.

The myriad of systems, platforms and business models currently available to the user community pose a variety of usability problems and challenges for information professionals and digital content service providers.

Usability of e-books

A number of studies (see for example, Dillon, 2001a, 2001b; Hughes and Buchanan, 2001; Langston, 2003; Bailey, 2006; Borchert et al., 2009) have focused specifically on the usability of e-books or digital books. Some researchers (see for example, Dillon, 2001a, 2001b; Christianson, 2005; Christianson and Aucoin, 2005; Nicholas et al. 2008) have investigated the spread of usage across titles in e-book collections; in all these studies, the results show a similar pattern, with most usage concentrated in a few high-use titles while for the majority of titles there was little or no use. Nicholas, Rowlands and Jamali (2010) noted that 45% of the use for one collection was generated by 'three to six year old' books. This shows that the use of digital books is not limited to new books only.

Grigson (2009) commented that a better understanding of the patterns of e-book usage requires a richer set of quantitative data than is available from current vendor reports. The JISC (2009) e-book national e-book observatory project aimed to fill this gap; the project studied online usage of e-books for 13 months – from November 2007 to December 2008 – involving 127 higher education institutions in the UK. The project was based on an understanding that there is a demand from UK higher education institutions for course texts including textbooks in digital format, and that there is an urgent need to know what users want in order to be prepared for meeting these demands.

The earlier JISC e-book study (Higher Education Consultancy Group, 2006) noted that students and teachers expect their university library to provide access to digital books to support their studies. This corroborates the JISC (2009, 19) e-book observatory study, which noted that digital books 'enable students and staff to fit work and study flexibly into their busy lifestyles'. Caren Milloy, Head of Projects and JISC Collections, commented (2010) that 'e-books are helping turn students into researchers'.

Emerging access and business models

A variety of access tools and new business models have appeared recently for access to e-books that will have a profound impact on the access and usability of digital content. All major e-book readers like Amazon Kindle, Sony e-book reader and Apple iPod/iPad have specific business models for providing access to e-book collections. Keeping in view that users often do not want to be tied to a specific reading device and the corresponding business model, and that it would be easy for publishers to set their own prices for each specific product, Google has come up with a new technology and business model called 'One Pass' (Google One Pass, 2011):

> Google One Pass is a payment system that enables publishers to set the terms for access to their digital content. It offers purchase-once, view-anywhere functionality, so users can view the content they buy across all of their devices.

However, for a user – for example, a university student or academic – the required information may come from a variety of digital information products and services or channels, and some of the content may be available for free while for others an appropriate registration and payment mechanism has to be set. Nevertheless, the access process should be smooth and transparent, and the user should not be required to move back and forth from one service provider or channel to another and follow a different access and use protocol for every stage of a transaction. Chowdhury (2009a, 2009b) presented details of such a system in two international conferences in 2009. Figure 10.1 shows the skeleton of a simple online information access system for academic users that will allow access to granular content coming from a variety of digital information sources and channels. The system will have in-built mechanisms for authentication and payment for fee-based (prices) content and at the same time provide access to free content, local or remote. The system will allow publishers or content creators set their own terms of

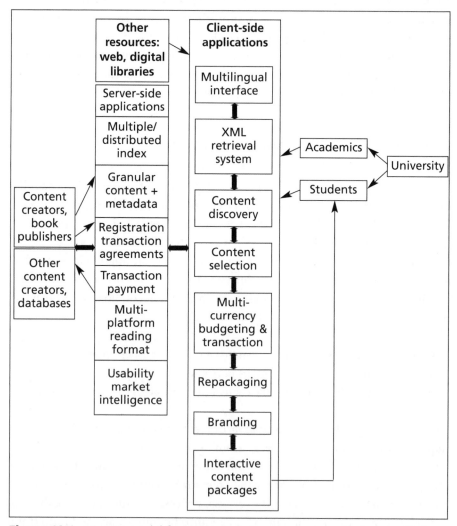

Figure 10.1 *A new model for access to heterogeneous content on multiple platforms*

access – fee-based, price-based or free access, tiered or variable price mechanisms and so on – and the system will generate market intelligence through log analyses that can be used to adjust the prices and/or the quality of service.

Social challenges: the digital divide and information skills

As discussed earlier in this book (Chapter 9), usability of digital information products and services is greatly influenced by social factors such as the digital divide and digital and information skills. Mossberger, Tolbert and Stansbury (2003) observed that the digital divide and usability are inherently linked in a vicious circle: without access users are not able to develop the required skills, and without skills they are unable to properly access and use digital information.

The overall digital information scenario in general, and usability of information products and services in particular, are significantly influenced by the widening gap between the younger generation, often called the Google generation or digital natives, and the rest of the population in their use and adoption of the internet and ICT in everyday life. Those in the Google generation can use and adapt to the emerging internet and mobile technologies better than older people, and more importantly they consider the web and social networks are the most important, if not the only, source of information. Consequently, these users' highly developed and adaptable skills in internet and mobile technologies, and high degree of dependence on the web and social networks for obtaining information of all kinds, will have an impact on the usability of online information products and services. Fortunately overall trends show that growing numbers of people across generations are becoming increasingly engaged with ICT, internet and mobile technologies. Many researchers believe that the gap between the Google generation and the rest of today's society in their use of the internet and ICT is not as big as it is often perceived; see for example, Rowlands et al., 2008; Gunter, Rowlands and Nicholas, 2009; and Selwyn, 2009. Rowlands et al. (2008) pointed out that, contrary to popular belief, the ubiquitous presence of the internet and ICT in the life of the younger generation does not result in improved information retrieval, information seeking or evaluation skills. Selwyn (2009) reminded us that we should remain especially mindful of the wider political and ideological agendas underlying the persistence of the digital native discourse in society.

Conclusion

Several research activities targeted at improving the usability of digital information services took place at the end of the 2000s, and some exist in 2011; seeing these changes in the digital world it is clear that digital libraries will be a ubiquitous tool in our everyday lives and activities in future. However, it is not clear what the nature or content of the new and emerging digital library will be, and what terms of reference it will have for access and use. Will it be like the flexible Google One Pass system, providing access to all kinds of digital books to read on a user-defined device, with the publisher offering different prices and terms of access for different devices? Or will it be accessed through a variety of the devices and business models that currently prevail? What will happen to the electronic journals and databases and aggregator services? Will the current range of usability studies, as discussed in different parts of this book, be able to influence the digital content marketplace? One can see that this is already happening: many usability studies have established that users prefer a one-window access to digital content and do not want to be tied up with a particular reading device. Is Google One Pass a new service in response to these studies?

Some publishers are beginning to break away from the traditional bundled model of publication where a book comprises several chapters, and a chapter comprises several long sections. Some publishers are coming up with a model of publishing books that are divided into small units, which can easily be accessed and read on small handheld devices. Research also shows that parallel to commercial information products and services, open access information is becoming increasingly common in the digital information world. Perhaps a model providing a one-stop shop access to all kinds of digital content, similar to the one shown earlier in this chapter (Figure 10.1), will be a viable alternative in the near future.

Finally, the climate change issue, as in any other field, will also have a significant impact on the digital information market and the usability of information. Research on climate change and the digital information world is just beginning (see for example Chowdhury, 2010), but this will pave the way for the development of future digital information services that are both economically and environmentally sustainable.

References

Anand, S. S. and Mobasher, B. (2005) Intelligent Techniques for Web Personalization.

In Mobasher, B. and Anand, S. S. (eds), *Intelligent Techniques for Web Personalization*, Lecture Notes in Artificial Intelligence 3169, Springer-Verlag, 1–36, http://maya.cs.depaul.edu/,mobasher/papers/am-itwp-springer05.pdf.

Bailey, T. P. (2006) Electronic Book Usage at a Master's Level I University: a longitudinal study, *Journal of Academic Librarianship*, **32** (1) 52–9.

Billsus, D. and Pazzani, M. J. (2000) User Modelling for Adaptive News Access, *User Modelling and User-adapted Interaction*, **10**, 147–80.

Borchert, M., Hunter, A., Macdonald D. and Tittel, C. (2009) A Study on Student and Staff Awareness, Acceptance and Usage of E-Books at Two Queensland Universities, http://eprints.usq.edu.au/4876/.

Borgman, C. L., Smart, L. J., Millwood, K. A., Finley, J. R., Champeny, L., Gilliland, A. J. and Leazer, G. H. (2005) Comparing Faculty Information Seeking in Teaching and Research: implications for the design of digital libraries, *Journal of the American Society for Information Science*, **56** (6), 636–57.

Bunkell, J. and Dyas-Correia, S. (2009) E-Books vs. Print: which is the better value?, *Serials Librarian*, **56** (1–4), 215–19.

Chowdhury, G. (2010) Carbon Footprint of the Knowledge Sector: what's the future?, *Journal of Documentation*, **66** (6), 934–46.

Chowdhury, G. G. (2004) Access and Usability Issues of Scholarly Electronic Publications. In Gorman, G. E. and Rowland, F. (eds), *Scholarly Publishing in an Electronic Era: International Yearbook of Library and Information Management, 2004/2005*, Facet Publishing, 77–98.

Chowdhury, G. G. (2009a) Towards the Conceptual Model of a Content Service Network. In *Globalizing Academic Libraries Vision 2020: proceedings of the International Conference on Academic Libraries, Delhi, Oct. 5–8*, Delhi Mittal Publications, 215–20.

Chowdhury, G. G. (2009b) Towards a New Service Model for the Content Supply Chain, [paper given at the] *Seventh Book Conference, University of Edinburgh*, 16–18 December 2009, http://2009.booksandpublishing.com/sessions/index.html.

Christianson, M. (2005) Patterns of Use of Electronic Books, *Library Collections Acquisitions and Technical Services*, **29** (4), 351–63.

Christianson, M. and Aucoin, M. (2005) Electronic or Print Books: which are used?, *Library Collections, Acquisitions and Technical Services*, **29** (1), 71–81.

Content Complete Ltd and OnlyConnect Consultancy (2009) *Study on the Management and Economic Impact of e-Textbook Business Models on Publishers, e-Book Aggregators and Higher Education Institutions: phase one report* (public version).

Dillon, D. (2001a) E-Books: the University of Texas experience, part 1, *Library Hi-Tech*, **19** (2) 113–24.

Dillon, D. (2001b) E-Books: the University of Texas experience, part 2, *Library Hi-Tech*, **19** (4) 350–62.

Dobreva, M. and Chowdhury, S. (2010) A User-Centric Evaluation of the Europeana Digital Library. In Chowdhury, G., Khoo, C. and Hunter, J. (eds), *[Proceedings of] the Role of Digital Libraries in a Time of Global Change, 12th International Conference on Asia-Pacific Digital Libraries, ICADL 2010, Gold Coast, Australia, June 21–25,* 148–57.

Fan, W., Gordon, M. D. and Pathak, P. (2005) Effective Profiling of Consumer Information Retrieval Needs: a unified framework and empirical comparison, *Decision Support Systems*, **40** (2), 213–33.

Frias-Martinez, E., Magoulas, G. D., Chen, S. Y. and Macredie, R. D. (2006) Automated User Modeling for Personalized Digital Libraries, *International Journal of Information Management*, **26** (3), 234–48.

Gibb, F. (2002) Resource Selection and Data Fusion for Multimedia International Digital Libraries: an overview of the MIND project. In *Proceedings of the EU/NSF All Projects Meeting, Rome, 25–26 March, ERCIM-02-W02, ERCIM, Sophia-Antipolis,* 51–6.

Google One Pass (2011) www.google.com/landing/onepass/.

Grigson, A. (2009) Evaluating Business Models for E-books Through Usage Data Analysis: a case study from the University of Westminster, *Journal of Electronic Resources Librarianship*, **21** (1), 62–74.

Gunter, B., Rowlands, I. and Nicholas, D. (2009) *The Google Generation: are ICT innovations changing information-seeking behaviour?*, Chandos Publishing.

Hicks, D. (2003) Supporting Personalization and Customization, *Computers in Industry*, **52** (1), 71–9.

Higher Education Consultancy Group (2006) *A Feasibility Study on the Acquisition of EBooks by HE Libraries and the Role of JISC*, www.jiscebooksproject.org/faq-links/ebwgreports/e-bookacquisition.

Hughes, C. A. and Buchanan, N. L. (2001) Use of Electronic Monographs in the Humanities and Social Sciences, *Library Hi Tech*, **19** (4), 368–75.

JISC (2007) *What is Deep Log Analysis?*, National E-Books Observatory Project, JISC, www.jiscebooksproject.org/deep-log-analysis/what-is-deep-log-analysis.

JISC (2009) *Key Findings and Recommendations: final report, November 2009*, National E-Books Observatory Project, JISC, www.jiscebooksproject.org/wp-content/JISC-e-books-observatory-final-report-Nov-09.pdf.

Jones, C., Zenios, M. and Griffiths, J. (2004) Academic Use of Digital Resources: disciplinary differences and the issue of progression. In *Proceedings of the Networked Learning Conference*, www.shef.ac.uk/nlc2004/Proceedings/symposia/.

Koychev, I. and Schwab, L. (2000) *Adapting to Drifting User's Interests*, www.cs.ubc.ca/,mike/papers/KoySch00.pdf.

Langston, M. (2003) The California State University E-Book Pilot Project: implications for cooperative collection development, *Library Collections, Acquisitions and Technical Services*, **27** (1), 19–32.

McCallum, A. and Nigam, K. (1998) *A Comparison of Event Models for Naïve Bayes Text Classification*, www.cs.cmu.edu/,knigam/papers/multinomial-aaaiws98.pdf.

Meyyappan, N., Chowdhury, G. G. and Foo, S. (2001) Use of a Digital Work Environment (DWE) Prototype to Create a User-Centred University Digital Library, *Journal of Information Science*, **27** (4), 249–64.

Meyyappan, N., Foo, S. and Chowdhury, G. G. (2004) Design of a Task-Based Digital Library for the Academic Community, *Journal of Documentation*, **60** (4), 449–75

Milloy, C. (2010) Why E-Books Mean Business, *Research Information*, **47**, April/May, 17.

Mossberger, K., Tolbert, C. J. and Stansbury, M. (2003) *Virtual Inequality: beyond the digital divide*, Georgetown University Press.

Nicholas, D., Rowlands, I. and Jamali, H. (2010) E-Textbook Use, Information Seeking Behaviour and its Impact: case study business and management, *Journal of Information Science*, **36** (2), 263–80.

Nicholas, D., Rowlands, I., Clark, D., Huntington, P., Jamali, H. R. and Ollé, C. (2008) UK Scholarly E-Book Usage: a landmark survey, *Aslib Proceedings: New Information Perspectives*, **60** (4), 311–34.

Nielsen, J. (1993) *Usability Engineering*, Academic Press.

OECD (2008) *Measuring the Impacts of ICT Using Official Statistics*, Directorate for Science Technology and Industry, Committee for Information, Computer and Communications Policy, DSTI/ICCP/IIS(2007)1/FINAL.

Pool, R. (2010) Open to Debate, *Research Information*, **47**, 12–14.

Renda, M. E. and Straccia, U. (2005) A Personalized Collaborative Digital Library Environment: a model and an application, *Information Processing & Management, An Asian Digital Libraries Perspective*, **41** (1), 5–21.

Rowlands, I., Nicholas, D., Williams, P., Huntington, P. and Fieldhouse, M. (2008) The Google Generation: the information behaviour of the researcher of the future, *Aslib Proceedings: New Information Perspectives*, **60** (4), 209–310.

Saulnier, A. and Viaud, M.-L. (2009) *Evaluation Report of the Usability of the Europeana Website*, www.version1.europeana.eu/c/document_library/get_file?uuid=ae1d74de-29c1-463c-887e-a6bc6ee0ed7a&groupId=10602.

Selwyn, N. (2009) The Digital Native: myth and reality, *Aslib Proceedings: New*

Information Perspectives, **61** (4), 364–79.

Segev, E. (2010) *Google and the Digital Divide: the bias of online knowledge*, Woodhead Publishing.

Shahabi, C. and Chen, Y.-S. (2003) Web Information Personalization: challenges and approaches. In *Proceedings of Databases in Networked Information Systems: 3rd International Workshop, DNIS 2003, Aizu, Japan, September 22–24*, Lecture Notes in Computer Science, Springer, 5–15.

Skykes, J., Dobreva, M., Birrell, D., McCulloch, E., Ruthven, I., Ünal, Y. and Feliciati, P. (2010) Focus on End Users: eye-tracking analysis for digital libraries. In Lalmas, M. et al. (eds), *Research and Advanced Technology for Digital Libraries, 14th European Digital Library Conference, Glasgow, 14–16 Sept*, Lecture Notes in Computer Science 6273, 510–13.

Wu, S., Crestani, F. and Gibb, F. (2004) New Methods for Results Merging in Distributed Information Retrieval. In *Proceedings of the ACM SIGIR 2003 Workshop on Distributed Information Retrieval, Toronto, Canada, August*, Lecture Notes in Computer Science 2924, Springer-Verlag, 84–100.

Index